CHRISTIAN APOLOGETIC EVANGELISM
Reaching Hearts with the Art of Persuasion

Edward D. Andrews

CHRISTIAN APOLOGETIC EVANGELISM

Reaching Hearts with the Art of Persuasion

Edward D. Andrews

Christian Publishing House

Cambridge, Ohio

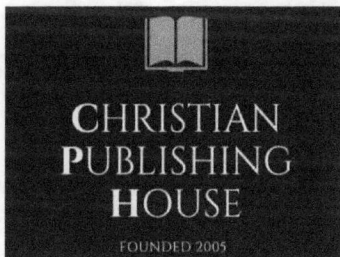

CHRISTIAN
PUBLISHING
HOUSE

FOUNDED 2005

support@christianpublishers.org

CHRISTIAN APOLOGETIC EVANGELISM: Reaching Hearts with the Art of Persuasion by Edward D. Andrews

ISBN-10: 1945757752

ISBN-13: 978-1945757754

Table of Contents

Edward D. Andrews

Preface

This book, *Christian Apologetic Evangelism: Reaching Hearts with the Art of Persuasion*, was written to equip believers with the understanding and conviction necessary to defend and proclaim the truth of the gospel in a world that has grown increasingly skeptical, relativistic, and hostile toward biblical faith. The purpose is not merely academic; it is deeply spiritual and evangelistic. The goal of apologetics is not to win arguments but to win souls—to reach hearts as well as minds, to persuade with truth expressed through love, and to glorify Jehovah by faithfully proclaiming His Word.

The modern Christian faces challenges far greater in scope and intensity than perhaps at any other time in recent memory. False ideologies, moral confusion, and the decay of objective truth have weakened the foundation of society and infiltrated even the visible church. Many have exchanged conviction for compromise, reason for emotion, and divine revelation for human speculation. Yet, amid this darkness, the light of God's truth still shines, unbroken and unchanging. The Bible remains the inspired, inerrant, and infallible Word of God—the final authority for faith and life. It is upon this unshakable foundation that this book stands.

True Christian apologetics must be rooted in Scripture, governed by sound reason, and guided by compassion. The believer is called not only to *know* what he believes but *why* he believes it—and to communicate that truth with clarity and conviction. The apostle Paul wrote, "We destroy arguments and every lofty thing raised up against the knowledge of God, and we take every thought captive to the obedience of Christ" (2 Corinthians 10:5). This command forms the heart of apologetic evangelism: the unyielding defense of truth coupled with the loving persuasion of those held captive by falsehood.

This book is designed to help readers develop both the mind and the heart of an apologist. It explores classical, evidential, presuppositional, and experiential approaches to defending the faith, demonstrating how each contributes to the unified mission of presenting Christianity as both rationally true and experientially real. It also provides practical guidance on how to evangelize effectively by imitating the perfect example of Jesus Christ and the faithful example of the Apostle Paul. Both men combined divine truth with human compassion, speaking with boldness yet always motivated by love for the lost.

Every page of this work has been written with the conviction that the Scriptures alone are sufficient to guide and govern both doctrine and method. The evangelist and apologist must rely wholly upon the power of the Word and the providence of God. While persuasive reasoning and careful study are essential, only Jehovah can open the heart to receive the truth. Therefore, prayer and humility are as vital to apologetics as logic and evidence.

This volume also seeks to restore confidence in the rationality of faith. Christianity is not irrational or anti-intellectual; it is the only worldview that makes sense of reality. The God of Scripture is the Author of both reason and revelation. The Christian need never fear the questions of the skeptic, for every challenge, when examined in the light of God's Word, ultimately confirms the truth of the faith once delivered to the holy ones.

The reader is encouraged to approach this book not as a collection of abstract theories but as a call to action. Every believer is an ambassador for Christ and a defender of truth. Whether in the home, workplace, or public arena, each Christian bears the responsibility to "shine as lights in the world, holding fast the word of life" (Philippians 2:15–16). Apologetics is not a discipline reserved for scholars—

it is the duty and privilege of every follower of Christ who desires to make His truth known.

May this book strengthen your conviction, deepen your understanding, and inspire you to engage the world with both courage and compassion. Let every argument, every defense, and every act of persuasion be carried out for the glory of Jehovah and the salvation of those still walking in darkness. For in the end, apologetics and evangelism are not separate pursuits—they are united in one mission: to exalt the truth of God in Christ and to bring others into His marvelous light.

Edward D. Andrews

Author of over 220 books and Chief Translator of the Updated American Standard Version

Edward D. Andrews

INTRODUCTION

The Christian faith stands upon a foundation that is both historical and eternal—rooted in divine revelation, confirmed by reason, and demonstrated through transformed lives. Yet, in a world dominated by skepticism, moral relativism, and intellectual pride, the proclamation of that faith requires more than zeal; it requires understanding. It requires believers who can communicate truth with both clarity and conviction—who can defend the gospel without compromise and share it with compassion. This is the purpose of *Christian Apologetic Evangelism: Reaching Hearts with the Art of Persuasion.*

Christian apologetics and evangelism are not separate disciplines but two dimensions of one divine commission. Apologetics is the defense of the faith; evangelism is the proclamation of that faith. Together, they form the full expression of Christian witness—reasoning from the truth of Scripture to the salvation found in Jesus Christ. The apologist clears away the intellectual obstacles that hinder belief, while the evangelist invites the hearer to respond to the truth in repentance and faith. When united, these two aspects create a powerful and balanced ministry that both convinces the mind and converts the heart.

From the earliest days of the church, believers have been called to defend the truth. The apostles reasoned with skeptics, debated philosophers, and answered objections from false religions. Yet they did so not merely to win arguments but to lead people to Christ. Their defense was rooted in love and expressed through persuasion. This balance of truth and compassion is the essence of Christian apologetic evangelism.

Today's believer faces an increasingly hostile culture—one that denies absolute truth, dismisses moral authority, and distorts the meaning of faith. Secularism, relativism, and religious pluralism have created a climate of confusion, where the claims of Christianity are often misrepresented or ignored. Many Christians feel intimidated or ill-equipped to respond to the challenges of atheism, humanism, and false religion. Yet, Scripture commands every follower of Christ to be ready to give a reason for the hope within them, and to do so with gentleness and respect.

This book is written to meet that need. It presents a comprehensive yet accessible guide . to understanding and practicing apologetics as an integral part of evangelism. It seeks to demonstrate that defending the faith is not the task of scholars alone but the responsibility of every believer who desires to live faithfully before Jehovah and bear witness to His truth.

The reader will find throughout these chapters a progression that reflects the logical and spiritual flow of apologetic reasoning and evangelistic ministry. It begins by explaining the **need for apologetics**—why defending the faith is essential in a world filled with error and deception. It then presents the **argument of apologetics**, outlining the twelve foundational propositions that flow logically from the reality of truth to the authority of Scripture. From there, it examines **classical, experiential, and presuppositional apologetics**, showing how each approach complements the others in building a comprehensive defense of Christianity.

Following these foundational discussions, the book turns to the practical application of apologetics in evangelism. These sections—**Reaching Hearts with the Art of Persuasion, Developing the Art of Effective Evangelism, Imitating Jesus When Evangelizing**, and **Imitating the Apostle Paul When Evangelizing**— illustrate how truth, reason, and compassion unite in the life of the believer to reach others with the gospel. The focus moves from philosophy to practice, from argument to appeal, showing how apologetics becomes evangelism when truth is expressed through love.

Throughout the book, the emphasis remains on the authority of Scripture as the final and infallible standard for truth. Human reason is a tool, but divine revelation is the foundation. Apologetics must never elevate philosophy above the Word of God; rather, it must bring every human thought captive to the obedience of Christ. The same principle governs evangelism: success is not measured by numerical response but by faithfulness to the message and reliance upon the power of God.

The apologetic methods discussed here—classical, evidential, experiential, and presuppositional—are not competing systems but complementary expressions of the same truth. Each reflects a different facet of God's revelation. Classical Apologetics begins with the rational proof of God's existence and the reliability of Scripture. Evidential Apologetics points to the historical and empirical evidence confirming the resurrection and the divine origin of the Bible. Experiential Apologetics appeals to the transformative power of the gospel in the believer's life. Presuppositional Apologetics reveals that only the biblical worldview provides the foundation for reason, morality, and truth itself. Together, they provide a complete defense and presentation of the faith once delivered to the holy ones.

Yet apologetics without evangelism is incomplete. Defending truth without proclaiming it is like guarding treasure without sharing it. The Christian must not only silence falsehood but also speak life. The goal is not intellectual victory but spiritual transformation. The apologist must remember that behind every argument stands a soul created in the image of God, in need of reconciliation with Him.

Evangelism, therefore, must reflect both the wisdom and compassion of Christ. Jesus, the Master Evangelist, spoke truth with authority yet touched hearts with mercy. He reasoned from Scripture, exposed hypocrisy, and invited sinners to repentance. His method combined perfect truth and perfect love. The Apostle Paul followed that same model— reasoning from Scripture, persuading by logic, and pleading with tears. He spoke as one who was both convinced and compassionate, declaring, "Knowing the fear of the Lord, we persuade men" (2 Corinthians 5:11).

To imitate Jesus and Paul in evangelism is to unite intellect with empathy, conviction with compassion, and truth with tenderness. It means to reason clearly, speak courageously, and live consistently. It requires both the mind of a theologian and the heart of a shepherd.

Christian Apologetic Evangelism calls believers back to that biblical balance. It teaches that apologetics is not a cold intellectual exercise but a spiritual discipline rooted in love for God and others. It shows that the defense of the faith is an act of worship, an offering of reason and devotion to the Author of truth. It reminds the reader that persuasion, when guided by humility and compassion, becomes a powerful tool in the hands of God for the salvation of souls.

The reader is invited to study these pages not merely for information but for transformation. May this work inspire you to think deeply, speak wisely, and live faithfully. May it equip you to defend the truth with courage and proclaim it with compassion. And above all, may it move you to glorify Jehovah through every conversation, every act of witness, and every effort to reach the lost. For evangelism is not only the duty of the believer—it is the heartbeat of the Christian life.

APOLOGETICS 1
Introduction to Christian Apologetics

Christian Apologetics is the reasoned defense of the Christian faith, derived from the Greek term *apologia*, meaning "a defense" or "a reasoned statement." It involves both affirming the truth of Christianity and refuting objections raised against it. The Apostle Peter urged believers to "sanctify Christ as Lord in your hearts, always being ready to make a defense to everyone who asks you to give an account for the hope that is in you, but with gentleness and respect" (1 Peter 3:15). This verse serves as the cornerstone of Christian Apologetics. The purpose of apologetics is not to replace faith with intellectualism but to demonstrate that faith in Christ is both rational and evidentially grounded. It strengthens believers, removes obstacles to belief for skeptics, and glorifies God by showing the coherence of His revealed truth.

Apologetics stands as a vital discipline within Christian theology because Christianity makes objective truth claims about God, humanity, sin, and salvation through Jesus Christ. It asserts that truth is absolute and that the Scriptures, as inspired by God, are the ultimate authority in all matters of faith and conduct. The defense of the faith, therefore, involves explaining and demonstrating that the Bible's teachings correspond to reality—historically, morally, and spiritually. The apologist's task is to show that belief in the Christian worldview is not only reasonable but the only coherent explanation for the world, human existence, and morality.

The Biblical Foundation of Apologetics

The foundation for apologetics is explicitly laid in Scripture. Jesus Himself defended truth claims about His identity and mission (John 5:31–47; 8:46). The Apostle Paul reasoned from the Scriptures in synagogues and marketplaces, persuading both Jews and Greeks that Jesus is the Messiah (Acts 17:2–3, 17; 18:4). In Acts 17:22–31, Paul addressed the philosophers of Athens, appealing to both general revelation and specific biblical truth to demonstrate the reality of God and the resurrection of Christ.

Scripture repeatedly calls believers to guard sound doctrine and refute error. Titus 1:9 says that an overseer must "be holding firmly to the faithful word which is in accordance with the teaching, so that he will be able both to exhort in sound doctrine and to refute those who contradict." Jude 3 exhorts

Christians to "contend earnestly for the faith that was once for all handed down to the holy ones." These passages establish that apologetics is not optional for the Christian; it is an integral part of discipleship and evangelism.

Apologetics also honors Jehovah by showing His truth to be consistent with reason. While human reason is not a substitute for revelation, it is a gift from God meant to be used in submission to His Word. Thus, apologetics demonstrates that faith and reason are allies, not enemies. Christianity invites investigation because it rests upon verifiable historical events and an internally coherent worldview.

The Purpose and Necessity of Christian Apologetics

The purpose of Christian Apologetics is threefold: to strengthen believers, to answer skeptics, and to evangelize the lost. For believers, apologetics reinforces confidence in Scripture by providing historical, logical, and moral reasons for faith. When confronted with doubt, misunderstanding, or false teaching, believers are equipped to stand firm on the unchanging truth of God's Word. For skeptics, apologetics removes intellectual barriers to faith, exposing the inconsistency of unbelief and presenting the reasonableness of Christianity. For evangelism, apologetics clarifies the gospel and invites repentance and faith in Christ by demonstrating that the message is credible, historically grounded, and divinely revealed.

In today's world, where relativism, materialism, and atheism dominate, apologetics is more crucial than ever. The claim that "truth is relative" contradicts the biblical reality that truth is objective and defined by God. Jesus declared, "I am the way, and the truth, and the life; no one comes to the Father except through Me" (John 14:6). Such an exclusive claim demands defense in a culture that rejects absolute truth. Apologetics exposes the self-refuting nature of relativism and demonstrates that all people live as though truth is absolute, even when they deny it.

The modern apologist must also engage with naturalism—the belief that everything can be explained by physical causes alone. Christianity affirms that creation bears witness to its Creator. Psalm 19:1 states, "The heavens are telling of the glory of God; and the expanse is declaring the work of His hands." Paul reinforces this in Romans 1:20, explaining that God's invisible attributes are "clearly seen, being understood through what has been made, so that they are without excuse." Apologetics, therefore, reveals that the order, complexity, and purpose in the universe point unmistakably to Jehovah's intelligent design.

The Relationship Between Faith and Reason

Faith in Christianity is not a blind leap into the dark but a confident trust in the light of God's revelation. Hebrews 11:1 defines faith as "the assurance of things hoped for, the conviction of things not seen." Faith involves trust in what God has revealed, grounded in evidence that He has provided through His Word, fulfilled prophecy, miracles, and historical reality.

Reason, rightly used, operates under the authority of Scripture. God created humanity with rational capacity, reflecting His own logical and orderly nature. As such, reason helps believers interpret Scripture accurately (using the Historical-Grammatical method) and evaluate arguments against the faith. However, reason must never stand in judgment over revelation. Instead, it serves revelation by clarifying, explaining, and defending it.

The Apostle Paul's method of reasoning with unbelievers illustrates this balance. He engaged both Jews and Gentiles through evidence, logic, and Scripture, yet always pointing them to faith in Christ.

This demonstrates that apologetics bridges the mind and the heart: it persuades the intellect so that the will may respond to the truth.

The Historical-Grammatical Method and Apologetics

The proper interpretation of Scripture forms the backbone of Christian Apologetics. The Historical-Grammatical method seeks to understand the text as the original author intended, within its historical and linguistic context. This approach preserves the inerrancy and authority of Scripture by treating it as literal truth rather than allegory or myth. The apologist who adheres to this method avoids the pitfalls of liberal or critical theology, which often undermines biblical authority by questioning the supernatural or reinterpreting miracles symbolically.

When the Bible is approached historically and grammatically, its divine coherence becomes evident. Prophecies fulfilled precisely, such as those concerning the Messiah, confirm divine authorship. For instance, Isaiah 53 and Psalm 22, written centuries before Christ, describe His suffering and death with astonishing accuracy. The New Testament writers, guided by the Holy Spirit, attest that these were fulfilled in Jesus (Acts 8:32–35). The factual fulfillment of prophecy serves as one of the strongest evidences for the divine inspiration of Scripture.

The Major Categories of Apologetics

Apologetics can be broadly divided into three interrelated branches: philosophical, evidential, and biblical (or presuppositional). Philosophical apologetics addresses questions concerning truth, morality, and the existence of God. It shows that a theistic worldview provides the only rational foundation for meaning, morality, and human dignity. Evidential apologetics demonstrates the reliability of Christianity through historical and empirical evidence—particularly the life, death, and resurrection of Jesus Christ. Biblical or presuppositional apologetics begins with the authority of Scripture itself, asserting that all reasoning must presuppose God's revelation because He is the source of all truth and logic.

Each approach plays a vital role in defending the faith. Philosophical arguments establish the coherence of theism. Evidential arguments confirm Christianity's historical reliability. Presuppositional reasoning exposes the impossibility of unbelief by showing that all logic, morality, and truth presuppose the existence of Jehovah. Together, these branches form a comprehensive defense of biblical Christianity.

The Apologist's Character and Method

Effective apologetics requires not only intellectual rigor but spiritual integrity. The apologist must be committed to personal holiness, humility, and love for those he seeks to persuade. As Paul wrote in 2 Timothy 2:24–25, "The Lord's slave must not be quarrelsome, but be kind to all, able to teach, patient when wronged, with gentleness correcting those who are in opposition." The goal is not to win arguments but to win souls, leading others to repentance and truth.

The apologist must also rely on the power of God's Word. Hebrews 4:12 declares that "the word of God is living and active and sharper than any two-edged sword." The ultimate authority in apologetics is Scripture itself, not human intellect. Arguments may expose inconsistencies in unbelief, but only the Word of God, working through the Holy Spirit's power, can bring conviction and transformation. Therefore, apologetics and evangelism must remain inseparable.

The Continuing Relevance of Christian Apologetics

In every generation, challenges to the faith have arisen—whether from paganism, Islam, atheism, secular humanism, or false Christianity. Yet the truth of the gospel remains unshaken. The apologist today faces not only overt opposition but also subtle compromise within professing Christianity, where liberal theology and moral relativism have eroded confidence in Scripture. Apologetics stands as the defense of biblical authority against both external attacks and internal corruption.

Christian Apologetics continues to be essential because truth never changes, even as cultures and philosophies shift. The Christian worldview offers the only consistent explanation for the origin, meaning, morality, and destiny of humanity. It affirms that man was created in the image of God, fell into sin, and can be redeemed only through the atoning work of Christ. All other worldviews fail to account for the moral law written on the human heart or the historical reality of the resurrection.

Ultimately, Christian Apologetics proclaims that faith in Jesus Christ is rational, historical, and transformational. It shows that the God who revealed Himself through Scripture and the person of His Son is the same God who created the universe and sustains it by His power. In defending the faith, Christians bear witness to the living truth that sets men free.

APOLOGETICS 2 The Need for Apologetics

The necessity of Christian Apologetics arises from the unchanging reality that truth is under constant assault in a fallen world. From the beginning, Satan's strategy has been to question and distort God's Word. His first recorded words in Scripture—"Did God really say?" (Genesis 3:1)—set the pattern for all subsequent attacks on divine revelation. Every false philosophy, religion, or worldview that denies the authority and reliability of Scripture continues that same deception. Christian Apologetics, therefore, is not a luxury for intellectuals or theologians but a biblical command for all who confess Jesus Christ as Lord. The defense of the faith is vital because it safeguards truth, strengthens believers, and provides a rational witness to an unbelieving world.

The Apostle Peter's exhortation remains the foundational mandate for every Christian: "Sanctify Christ as Lord in your hearts, always being ready to make a defense to everyone who asks you to give an account for the hope that is in you, but with gentleness and respect" (1 Peter 3:15). This is not a suggestion; it is a divine imperative. Apologetics arises out of a sanctified heart, one fully devoted to Christ.

The believer who has yielded his mind and will to Jehovah must be ready to articulate and defend the reasons for his faith with both conviction and compassion.

The Spiritual Necessity of Apologetics

The first and most fundamental reason for apologetics is spiritual. Scripture declares that the entire world system lies under the influence of the wicked one (1 John 5:19). Satan blinds the minds of the unbelieving so that they will not see the light of the gospel of the glory of Christ (2 Corinthians 4:4). Therefore, the defense of the faith is not merely an intellectual exercise but a form of spiritual warfare. Paul wrote, "We are destroying speculations and every lofty thing raised up against the knowledge of God, and we are taking every thought captive to the obedience of Christ" (2 Corinthians 10:5).

The battle for truth is waged in the realm of ideas, philosophies, and moral reasoning. Apologetics exposes the lies of the enemy by confronting false ideologies with the truth of Scripture. It tears down intellectual strongholds built on unbelief, pride, and rebellion against God. Whether the challenge comes from atheism, humanism, materialism, or false religion, the apologist's duty is to bring every argument into submission to Christ's authority.

Apologetics is also necessary because of the human heart's deceitfulness. Jeremiah 17:9 declares, "The heart is more deceitful than all else and is desperately sick." Fallen humanity suppresses the truth of God in unrighteousness (Romans 1:18). Unbelievers do not reject Christianity for lack of evidence but because of a moral refusal to submit to divine authority. Therefore, apologetics confronts not only intellectual objections but the underlying moral rebellion that fuels them.

While the apologist presents evidence, logic, and reason, he understands that conviction and conversion come through the Holy Spirit operating through the Word of God. The apologist's role is to proclaim, clarify, and defend, while Jehovah Himself opens the heart to respond, as He did for Lydia in Acts 16:14.

The Biblical Mandate for Defending the Faith

Apologetics is commanded throughout Scripture. In addition to 1 Peter 3:15, Jude 3 instructs believers to "contend earnestly for the faith that was once for all handed down to the holy ones." The term "contend" (*epagonizomai*) conveys intense effort and perseverance in defending truth against distortion. Paul repeatedly warned of false teachers and deceptive doctrines that would arise within the church (Acts 20:29–30; 1 Timothy 4:1–2). He charged Timothy to "guard the good deposit" (2 Timothy 1:14) and to "preach the word; be ready in season and out of season; reprove, rebuke, exhort, with great patience and instruction" (2 Timothy 4:2).

These commands establish that defending the faith is inseparable from proclaiming it. The gospel must not only be announced but protected. The earliest Christians faced opposition from pagan philosophers, Jewish legalists, and Gnostic heretics. Yet, they defended the truth courageously, grounding their faith in the historical resurrection of Christ, the fulfillment of prophecy, and the divine authority of Scripture.

The Intellectual Necessity of Apologetics

Another reason for apologetics is intellectual integrity. Christianity is not based on blind faith but on evidence and revelation. The God who commands believers to love Him with all their heart also commands them to love Him with all their mind (Matthew 22:37). Faith and reason are not enemies;

they are complementary. True faith is strengthened by understanding, and understanding deepens faith.

The Christian worldview provides the only coherent foundation for truth, morality, meaning, and human dignity. Without God, there is no ultimate basis for moral obligation or rational order. Materialistic atheism cannot account for the immaterial realities that govern logic, ethics, and human consciousness. Apologetics demonstrates that belief in Jehovah is the precondition for knowledge itself. As Proverbs 1:7 declares, "The fear of Jehovah is the beginning of knowledge."

Apologetics also provides an intellectual safeguard against deception. False ideologies flourish when believers lack discernment. Paul warned the Colossians, "See to it that no one takes you captive through philosophy and empty deception, according to the tradition of men, according to the elementary principles of the world, rather than according to Christ" (Colossians 2:8). Apologetics equips the believer to identify, evaluate, and refute such philosophies by holding them up to the light of Scripture.

The Moral and Cultural Necessity of Apologetics

The need for apologetics extends beyond theological defense to moral and cultural preservation. As societies drift away from biblical truth, they lose the foundation for morality, justice, and human value. Modern culture's rejection of absolute truth, gender distinctions, and divine authority reveals the depth of its rebellion against God. Apologetics confronts this rebellion by affirming that truth is objective, moral law is grounded in God's character, and human beings possess worth because they are created in His image (Genesis 1:26–27).

When Christians fail to defend biblical morality, they allow ungodly ideologies to shape the culture. Silence in the face of moral confusion is complicity. Apologetics gives believers the tools to speak truth with clarity and conviction, showing that God's standards are not arbitrary but rooted in His righteous and loving nature. The moral decline of nations follows their rejection of divine revelation, and only a return to biblical truth can restore stability and purpose.

In the first century, the Roman Empire was characterized by idolatry, immorality, and spiritual blindness, yet Christianity triumphed through truth, not violence or compromise. The same must be true today. The apologist's task is to confront darkness with the light of the gospel and to show that the biblical worldview alone explains reality as it is.

The Evangelistic Necessity of Apologetics

Apologetics serves evangelism by removing obstacles that prevent unbelievers from hearing the gospel with understanding. While no one is argued into the Kingdom of God by reason alone, apologetics clears away misconceptions, exposes falsehoods, and prepares the soil for the seed of the Word. The Apostle Paul engaged in apologetic reasoning throughout his ministry. In Acts 17, he reasoned with Jews from the Scriptures, explaining and giving evidence that the Messiah had to suffer and rise from the dead. In the same chapter, he addressed Greek philosophers on Mars Hill, demonstrating that their "unknown god" was in fact the Creator who revealed Himself in Jesus Christ.

Paul's approach was not accommodation but confrontation with truth. He met people where they were intellectually but did not leave them there. He brought them face to face with the claims of Christ and the necessity of repentance. The effectiveness of apologetics lies not in intellectual victory but in leading others to salvation. The goal is not to win arguments but to win souls.

Evangelistic apologetics must therefore combine reason with compassion. The apologist who argues harshly or pridefully misrepresents the character of Christ. Peter emphasized gentleness and respect because the manner of defense is as important as the content. Apologetics without love is hollow, just as love without truth is powerless. The apologist's heart must burn with concern for the lost, desiring that all come to repentance and the knowledge of the truth (1 Timothy 2:4).

The Ecclesiastical Necessity of Apologetics

Within the church, apologetics preserves doctrinal purity and guards against heresy. False teachers, both ancient and modern, distort Scripture to promote human philosophies or worldly agendas. Paul warned that "the time will come when they will not endure sound doctrine, but wanting to have their ears tickled, they will accumulate for themselves teachers in accordance with their own desires" (2 Timothy 4:3). That time has clearly come. The church today faces internal compromise through liberal theology, prosperity teaching, mysticism, and cultural accommodation.

Apologetics protects the church by reaffirming the inerrancy, sufficiency, and authority of Scripture. It calls believers back to the pure teaching of God's Word, interpreted through the Historical-Grammatical method rather than human speculation. When doctrine is defended, the church is strengthened; when doctrine is neglected, the church becomes vulnerable to deception.

Moreover, apologetics fosters unity among believers by grounding their faith in truth rather than emotion or tradition. Sound doctrine provides stability, clarity, and confidence. It equips elders, teachers, and members alike to discern between truth and error. Thus, apologetics serves the health and growth of the body of Christ.

The Personal Necessity of Apologetics

Apologetics also serves a deeply personal role in the life of every believer. Many Christians struggle with doubts, questions, or confusion about their faith. Through study and defense of the truth, believers develop a deeper confidence in God's Word and a stronger relationship with Christ. Apologetics transforms uncertainty into conviction and fear into courage.

When believers understand *why* they believe, they are less likely to be shaken by opposition. Jesus described the wise man who built his house on the rock: "The rain fell, and the floods came, and the winds blew and slammed against that house; and yet it did not fall, for it had been founded on the rock" (Matthew 7:25). Apologetics lays that firm foundation, grounding the believer's faith on truth rather than emotion or circumstance.

Furthermore, personal apologetic study enhances worship. When Christians grasp the depth of God's wisdom revealed in creation, prophecy, and redemption, their reverence deepens. The defense of the faith leads to adoration of the Author of faith. The apologist who studies the evidence for God's existence, the historical reliability of Scripture, and the person of Christ cannot help but respond in praise and gratitude.

The Ultimate Goal of Apologetics

The ultimate goal of Christian Apologetics is not intellectual triumph but the glory of God. Every defense of the faith is an act of worship, testifying to the truthfulness and faithfulness of Jehovah. The apologist's aim is to magnify Christ by showing that His gospel is rational, historical, and morally superior to every competing worldview. The defense of truth honors the God of truth.

When Christians engage in apologetics with humility and faithfulness, they reflect the character of Christ, who is "the faithful and true witness" (Revelation 3:14). They participate in the divine mission of proclaiming light to those in darkness and demonstrating that belief in Jesus Christ is not only reasonable but necessary. In defending the truth, believers fulfill their calling as ambassadors of the Kingdom of God, standing firm amid a world of deception and proclaiming that "the word of our God stands forever" (Isaiah 40:8).

APOLOGETICS 3 Argument of Apologetics

The discipline of Christian Apologetics involves both the defense and the confirmation of the Christian faith through rational, evidential, and biblical argumentation. Among the various methods of apologetics—classical, evidential, cumulative, presuppositional—the **classical method** offers a clear, logical progression that demonstrates the truth of Christianity beginning from universally knowable truths about reality and reason, advancing step by step to the conclusion that the Bible is the inspired and inerrant Word of God. This approach reflects the way God has revealed Himself in both general and special revelation—first through creation and conscience, then through Scripture and the person of Jesus Christ.

The classical approach recognizes that reason and revelation are not antagonistic but harmonious. God, who is the Author of both, does not contradict Himself. Truth, therefore, is consistent and knowable because it reflects the nature of Jehovah, who is the God of truth (Deuteronomy 32:4; John 14:6). Each proposition in the argument builds upon the previous one, creating a coherent case for the truthfulness of Christianity as revealed in the Bible. The logic of apologetics thus moves from the general to the specific—from the nature of reality and reason to the existence of God, the person of Christ, and the authority of Scripture.

The Logical Progression of Classical Apologetics

The classical argument can be summarized in twelve interdependent propositions. Each builds upon what precedes it, forming a logical sequence that leads to the conclusion that Christianity is true and all competing systems of belief are false when they contradict it.

1. Truth About Reality Is Knowable

The foundation of all apologetics rests upon the affirmation that truth exists and can be known. Without truth, reasoning collapses, and all communication becomes meaningless. The denial of truth is self-defeating, for to claim that "truth cannot be known" is itself a truth-claim that assumes the very thing it denies. Scripture confirms that God created human beings with rational capacity and the ability to perceive truth. "The truth will make you free" (John 8:32). To know truth is to know reality as it actually is, corresponding to what God has revealed.

2. Opposites Cannot Both Be True

This is the law of non-contradiction, a principle foundational to all reasoning. It states that two contradictory statements cannot both be true in the same sense and at the same time. For example, it cannot be true that God exists and also true that God does not exist. Jehovah is a God of order and logic; therefore, His creation and revelation operate within the bounds of rational consistency. Isaiah 1:18 records God's invitation, "Come now, and let us reason together." Christianity alone stands consistently upon this logical foundation, whereas relativism and pluralism contradict themselves by affirming that mutually exclusive beliefs can all be true.

3. The Theistic God Exists

If truth exists and the law of non-contradiction is valid, then the existence of God can be demonstrated through rational and empirical evidence. The universe had a beginning, and whatever begins to exist must have a cause. This cause must be eternal, uncaused, and personal, possessing intelligence and power—attributes that belong solely to the theistic God revealed in Scripture. The creation declares God's existence (Psalm 19:1), and human conscience confirms it (Romans 2:14–15). Natural revelation, therefore, leads us to the conclusion that a personal, moral, transcendent Creator exists.

4. Miracles Are Possible

If a personal, all-powerful Creator exists, then miracles are possible. A miracle is not a violation of natural law but an intervention by the One who established those laws. Since God created the universe, He has authority over it and can act within it according to His sovereign will. The existence of God makes the possibility of miracles both rational and expected. In fact, miracles serve a divine purpose—to authenticate God's revelation and messengers.

5. Miracles Performed in Connection with a Truth Claim Are Acts of God to Confirm the Truth of God Through a Messenger of God

Miracles, when genuine, confirm divine authority. They are not random displays of power but purposeful acts to validate the truth of God's message. Moses' miracles confirmed Jehovah's deliverance of Israel from Egypt (Exodus 7–12). Elijah's miracles affirmed the supremacy of the true God over Baal (1 Kings 18). The miracles of Jesus verified His identity as the Messiah and Son of God. John wrote, "These have been written so that you may believe that Jesus is the Christ, the Son of God, and that believing you may have life in His name" (John 20:31).

6. The New Testament Documents Are Reliable

The reliability of the New Testament is foundational to knowing the historical Jesus and His teachings. The New Testament is the best-attested collection of ancient writings in existence. Over 5,800 Greek manuscripts confirm that its text is 99.99% accurate to the original autographs. Archaeology, early quotations by church fathers, and internal consistency all affirm its authenticity. The New Testament was written within the first century by eyewitnesses or those who had direct contact with eyewitnesses (Luke 1:1–4; 1 John 1:1–3). The historical and textual evidence overwhelmingly supports its credibility.

7. As Witnessed in the New Testament, Jesus Claimed to Be God

The Jesus of history explicitly claimed divine authority. He identified Himself as the Son of God, declared oneness with the Father (John 10:30), accepted worship (Matthew 14:33), forgave sins

(Mark 2:5–7), and applied divine titles to Himself such as "I AM" (John 8:58), which recalls Jehovah's self-identification in Exodus 3:14. His trial before the Sanhedrin confirmed that His claim to deity was the central issue leading to His execution (Mark 14:61–64). Jesus' claim to be God in the flesh is not an invention of later theology but a historical fact recorded by the earliest witnesses.

8. Jesus' Claim to Divinity Was Proven by a Unique Convergence of Miracles

Unlike any other figure in history, Jesus performed miracles that demonstrated authority over nature, disease, demons, and death. He turned water into wine (John 2:1–11), calmed storms (Mark 4:39), raised the dead (John 11:43–44), and healed multitudes. His greatest miracle—the resurrection—serves as the ultimate vindication of His divine identity. The resurrection was not a mere spiritual metaphor but a physical, historical event attested by over five hundred eyewitnesses (1 Corinthians 15:3–8). These miracles provide divine authentication of His person and message.

9. Therefore, Jesus Was God in Human Flesh

Given the reliability of the New Testament and the unique convergence of miracles confirming His claims, the conclusion follows logically that Jesus was who He said He was—God incarnate. John 1:14 declares, "The Word became flesh, and dwelt among us." In Jesus Christ, Jehovah entered human history in bodily form to redeem fallen mankind. This truth distinguishes Christianity from every other religion, for no other faith presents a God who became man to atone for sin.

10. Whatever Jesus (Who Is God) Affirmed as True Is True

Because Jesus is God, His words carry absolute authority. God cannot lie (Titus 1:2), and His Son spoke only truth. Jesus testified, "Heaven and earth will pass away, but My words will not pass away" (Matthew 24:35). Therefore, whatever Jesus affirmed—about Himself, about Scripture, about salvation, or about history—is true without error. To reject His words is to reject God Himself.

11. Jesus Affirmed That the Bible Is the Word of God

Jesus consistently affirmed the divine inspiration and authority of Scripture. He quoted the Old Testament as the very Word of God, declaring, "Scripture cannot be broken" (John 10:35). He validated the historical accuracy of Genesis (Matthew 19:4–5), the Mosaic authorship of the Law (Mark 7:10), and the prophetic authority of the prophets (Luke 24:27). Moreover, He promised His apostles that the Holy Spirit would guide them into all truth (John 16:13), ensuring the divine inspiration of the New Testament.

12. Therefore, It Is True That the Bible Is the Word of God and Whatever Is Opposed to Any Biblical Truth Is False

From these propositions, the conclusion follows with logical necessity. Since Jesus is God and affirmed the Bible as God's Word, the Scriptures possess divine authority and inerrancy. Therefore, any belief system or claim that contradicts the Bible is false. Christianity alone corresponds fully to reality, reason, and divine revelation.

The Application of the Argument

If it is true that the theistic God exists, that miracles are possible, that Jesus Christ is the Son of God, and that the Bible is the Word of God, then it logically follows that orthodox, biblical Christianity is true. All essential doctrines—such as the Trinity, the virgin birth, the substitutionary atonement, the bodily resurrection, and the second coming of Christ—are taught within Scripture and therefore possess divine authority.

This reasoning excludes the validity of all opposing worldviews. Because truth is exclusive and opposites cannot both be true, any religion that denies the doctrines of biblical Christianity is false insofar as it contradicts them. Islam denies the deity of Christ, Hinduism affirms pantheism, and Buddhism rejects the personal Creator altogether. These cannot coexist with biblical theism. As Paul declared, "There is one God, and one Mediator also between God and men, the man Christ Jesus" (1 Timothy 2:5).

This exclusivity is not arrogance but consistency. If Jehovah is the only true God and Jesus Christ is His Son, then to affirm another path to salvation is to deny the very truth God has revealed. Christianity is not one among many truths—it is the truth.

Apologetics demonstrates this not by emotional appeal but by rational and evidential proof grounded in Scripture and history.

The Strength of the Classical Argument

The twelve propositions of classical apologetics form a complete and rational framework that aligns with both divine revelation and human reason. It begins where all humans can engage—acknowledgment of truth, logic, and reality—and proceeds through evidence that points to God's existence and the truthfulness of His Word. The argument's strength lies in its cumulative nature: each point reinforces the next, building an unbreakable chain from philosophical foundation to biblical conclusion.

The believer who understands and employs this argument is equipped to answer questions from skeptics, encourage faith in doubters, and affirm confidence in Scripture among fellow believers. The classical method respects both the intellect and the soul, showing that faith in Christ is not contrary to reason but perfectly consistent with it.

Ultimately, the argument of apologetics points to the One who declared Himself "the way, and the truth, and the life" (John 14:6). To know truth is to know Christ, for all truth finds its source and fulfillment in Him. The apologist's role is to guide others through this logical and evidential path so that they, too, may come to the saving knowledge of the truth.

APOLOGETICS 4 Classical Apologetics

Classical Apologetics is the oldest and most systematic method of defending the Christian faith. It emphasizes the rational, philosophical, and evidential foundations of Christianity by moving in logical sequence from general revelation (truths about reality, logic, and God's existence) to special revelation (the divinity of Jesus Christ and the authority of Scripture). This approach rests on the conviction that Christianity is not only spiritually true but also intellectually defensible and logically consistent. The classical method assumes that truth can be known, reason is valid, and God's existence can be demonstrated. It seeks to show that faith in Christ is the most rational conclusion one can reach from an honest evaluation of all available evidence.

Classical Apologetics recognizes that God is the Author of both reason and revelation. Since Jehovah is a God of truth, all truth—whether discovered through creation, conscience, or Scripture—originates in Him. Therefore, there can be no contradiction between sound reasoning and divine revelation. The classical apologist begins with what can be known by reason and observation, then builds upon that foundation to demonstrate the supernatural truth revealed in the Bible.

The Foundation and Nature of Classical Apologetics

The classical approach rests upon two primary affirmations: first, that truth about reality is knowable; second, that the law of non-contradiction governs all thought and existence. To deny these truths is self-defeating. The apologist begins by establishing that truth corresponds to reality, meaning that what is true accurately represents the way things are. From there, the argument moves to the existence of a personal, moral, infinite Creator—Jehovah. Once God's existence is established, the possibility of miracles becomes both rational and expected.

The term *classical* derives from the method's historical lineage among the early Church Fathers and medieval Christian philosophers such as Justin Martyr, Irenaeus, Augustine, and Thomas Aquinas. Each of these figures used rational argumentation to defend Christian theism against paganism, heresy, and skepticism. Their reasoning reflected the biblical principle that "the fear of Jehovah is the beginning of knowledge" (Proverbs 1:7) and that believers must be ready to "make a defense" (1 Peter 3:15). Classical

Apologetics does not rest faith upon reason but demonstrates that reason, when rightly used, leads inevitably to the truth revealed in Scripture.

The Two-Step Structure of the Classical Method

The classical method proceeds through two broad steps that encompass a total logical progression of twelve key propositions (outlined more fully in the "Argument of Apologetics"). The first step establishes the foundation for theism; the second confirms Christianity as the one true revelation of the theistic God.

Step One: Theism is True.

The apologist begins by showing that truth exists and that opposites cannot both be true. From these philosophical foundations, he demonstrates that the existence of a personal, moral, eternal Creator is the only explanation for the universe's origin, order, and moral structure. This involves arguments from cosmology (cause and effect), teleology (design and purpose), morality (objective moral law), and contingency (dependence of finite beings on an uncaused being). Each of these demonstrates that the material universe cannot be self-existent or self-caused. It must have a transcendent cause—Jehovah, who is eternal, necessary, intelligent, and personal.

Step Two: Christianity is True.

Once the existence of God is established, the apologist moves to demonstrate that this God has revealed Himself specifically through Jesus Christ and the Bible. This step affirms the possibility of miracles, the reliability of the New Testament, the deity of Christ, and the authority of Scripture. Historical evidence confirms that Jesus performed supernatural acts that authenticated His message and person. His resurrection, witnessed by hundreds and recorded by multiple sources, stands as the ultimate verification of His divine identity. Because Jesus affirmed that the Bible is the Word of God, it follows that Scripture is divinely inspired and true in all it affirms.

The Philosophical Basis of Classical Apologetics

At its core, Classical Apologetics is grounded in the belief that logic and truth reflect the nature of God. The law of non-contradiction—that something cannot be both true and false in the same sense and at the same time—is not an arbitrary human convention but an expression of God's rational order. God cannot deny Himself or contradict His own nature (2 Timothy 2:13). Therefore, when the apologist employs logic, he is reflecting the image of God, who is the ultimate source of reason.

This philosophical grounding distinguishes Classical Apologetics from fideism (the view that faith has no rational basis) and from evidentialism (which often bypasses philosophical foundations). The classical method insists that before one can meaningfully discuss the evidence for miracles or the resurrection, one must first establish the framework in which such events are possible—the existence of a theistic God. This systematic progression ensures that the argument for Christianity is coherent and cumulative.

The Use of General Revelation

Classical Apologetics draws heavily from general revelation—the knowledge of God available through creation and conscience. Psalm 19:1–4 declares, "The heavens are telling of the glory of God; and the expanse is declaring the work of His hands." Likewise, Paul wrote, "Since the creation of the world His invisible attributes, His eternal power and divine nature, have been clearly seen, being understood through what has been made, so that they are without excuse" (Romans 1:20).

General revelation provides sufficient evidence for the existence of God, though it does not by itself convey the message of salvation. It demonstrates that belief in a Creator is the most rational explanation for the universe. Apologetics uses this natural knowledge as a foundation upon which the special revelation of Scripture builds. By affirming the reliability of general revelation, the apologist shows that reason and faith are complementary, both deriving from the same divine source.

The Historical Defense of Classical Apologetics

Throughout history, classical apologists have stood at the forefront of Christian thought. In the second century, Justin Martyr appealed to reason and prophecy to defend Christianity before pagan philosophers, arguing that Jesus fulfilled the messianic predictions of the Hebrew Scriptures. Augustine in the fourth century demonstrated that truth and morality depend on the existence of the eternal God. Thomas Aquinas, in the thirteenth century, formulated five logical proofs for God's existence, showing that reason and revelation converge in affirming divine truth.

During the Reformation, leaders such as John Calvin and later conservative theologians upheld the harmony between faith and reason while emphasizing the authority of Scripture. In modern times, defenders of classical apologetics have continued to demonstrate that Christian theism alone provides a coherent worldview that accounts for all aspects of human experience—logic, morality, meaning, and destiny.

The Central Role of the Resurrection

Within Classical Apologetics, the resurrection of Jesus Christ serves as the pivotal historical event confirming all of Christianity's truth claims. Once it is shown that a theistic God exists and miracles are possible, the resurrection becomes not only plausible but expected as God's validation of His Son. The resurrection stands at the intersection of history and theology—it is both a supernatural act and a verifiable historical occurrence.

The New Testament records multiple independent witnesses to the resurrection (1 Corinthians 15:3–8). The empty tomb, the transformation of the apostles, and the rise of the early church all testify to its reality. The resurrection confirms Jesus' deity, validates His teachings, and proves that the Bible's message of redemption is divinely authenticated. In the classical framework, this event moves the argument from abstract theism to the specific truth of Christianity.

The Defense of Scripture's Authority

Because Jesus affirmed the divine authority of Scripture, Classical Apologetics concludes that the Bible is the infallible Word of God. Jesus stated, "Scripture cannot be broken" (John 10:35), and in Matthew 5:18 declared that not "the smallest letter or stroke shall pass from the Law until all is accomplished." The New Testament writers, inspired by the Holy Spirit, echoed this conviction. Paul wrote, "All Scripture is God-breathed" (2 Timothy 3:16).

The reliability of the biblical text is confirmed through historical evidence, manuscript preservation, and fulfilled prophecy. No other ancient document approaches the New Testament's textual accuracy or the Old Testament's prophetic precision. Classical Apologetics uses these evidences to demonstrate that the Bible is not merely a human composition but the written revelation of the living God.

Strengths of Classical Apologetics

One of the primary strengths of Classical Apologetics is its systematic and cumulative nature. It builds truth upon truth, ensuring that each conclusion logically follows from the last. This structure provides a comprehensive worldview defense that engages both the intellect and the heart. It begins where skeptics can agree—reality, logic, and causality—and then leads them step by step to the necessity of divine revelation.

Another strength is its enduring relevance. In an age dominated by relativism, materialism, and atheism, Classical Apologetics reaffirms the objectivity of truth and the rational foundation of faith. It answers the skeptic's claim that Christianity is irrational by demonstrating that disbelief in God is, in fact, logically incoherent. Every worldview that denies the God of the Bible ultimately undermines its own basis for truth and meaning.

Furthermore, this method respects the biblical pattern of reasoning found in Scripture. The prophets appealed to evidence and logic to prove Jehovah's superiority over idols (Isaiah 41:21–24). Jesus reasoned with His opponents using Scripture and miracles as proof of His divine authority (John 5:36–

39). Paul used the same method in Acts 17, reasoning with the philosophers in Athens from general revelation to special revelation, concluding with the resurrection of Christ. Thus, Classical Apologetics follows the apostolic example.

Misunderstandings About Classical Apologetics

Critics sometimes claim that Classical Apologetics places too much emphasis on reason or human logic. However, this is a misunderstanding of its purpose. The classical apologist does not attempt to replace faith with logic but to show that faith is grounded in truth. Reason cannot save anyone; only the gospel can. Yet, reason can lead a person to recognize the necessity and coherence of faith. Faith is not irrational—it is the proper response to sufficient evidence revealed by God.

Another misunderstanding is that Classical Apologetics assumes that unbelievers can reason neutrally. The Bible teaches that the natural man resists the truth (1 Corinthians 2:14). Nevertheless, even fallen humanity retains the ability to recognize basic logical and moral truths, for the image of God, though marred, is not destroyed. Classical Apologetics appeals to this residual capacity for rational thought as a bridge to the gospel, while fully acknowledging that conversion requires divine illumination.

The Goal and Fruit of Classical Apologetics

The ultimate goal of Classical Apologetics is not intellectual victory but the glory of God through the vindication of His truth. By demonstrating the rational coherence of Christianity, the apologist removes stumbling blocks that prevent people from hearing the gospel with understanding. Apologetics serves evangelism by preparing the way for faith, showing that the Christian worldview alone corresponds to reality and satisfies both the intellect and the soul.

For believers, Classical Apologetics deepens confidence in Scripture and strengthens conviction amid opposition. It equips the Christian to respond intelligently and faithfully to challenges against the faith. It also cultivates worship, for the more one understands the unity of God's truth in reason, revelation, and history, the more one reveres the infinite wisdom of the Creator.

The classical method thus fulfills both the mandate of 1 Peter 3:15 and the spirit of Isaiah 8:13: "Sanctify Jehovah of hosts Himself; and let Him be your fear, and let Him be your dread." It sanctifies Christ as Lord in the heart and exalts His truth in the world.

APOLOGETICS 5
Experiential Apologetics

Experiential Apologetics focuses on the defense and confirmation of the Christian faith through the reality of personal and collective experience that corresponds with divine truth revealed in Scripture. While Classical and Evidential Apologetics rely primarily on reason and empirical evidence, Experiential Apologetics emphasizes the transformative power of Christianity as living proof of its truth. It demonstrates that Christianity is not merely a theoretical system of beliefs but a personal relationship with the living God—Jehovah—through Jesus Christ. This method argues that the inward witness of the Holy Spirit, the moral and spiritual transformation of believers, and the historical impact of Christianity all serve as experiential evidence for its divine origin.

Experiential Apologetics does not dismiss reason or evidence; rather, it complements them. It begins where people live—in the realm of human experience, emotion, conscience, and spiritual hunger—and shows that the Christian faith alone provides the true and satisfying explanation for the deepest needs of the human soul. Human beings are not merely rational creatures; they are moral and spiritual beings created in God's image, designed for fellowship with Him. Thus, the defense of the faith must also address the experiential dimension of life, for the gospel is not only credible but transformative.

The Biblical Basis for Experiential Apologetics

The Scriptures consistently affirm that God's truth is to be known not only intellectually but experientially. The psalmist declared, "Taste and see that Jehovah is good" (Psalm 34:8). This invitation is not to blind faith but to personal participation in the reality of God's goodness. Jesus promised, "If anyone is willing to do His will, he will know about the teaching, whether it is of God" (John 7:17). Faithful obedience brings experiential confirmation of divine truth.

Paul appealed to experience as a form of validation when he wrote to the Galatians, "Did you receive the Spirit by works of the Law, or by hearing with faith?" (Galatians 3:2). The transformation of their lives through the message of Christ was itself proof of the gospel's divine power. Similarly, in Romans 8:16, he affirmed, "The Spirit Himself bears witness with our spirit that we are children of God."

This inner witness does not replace Scripture but confirms it in the believer's life.

The apostles themselves grounded their faith in what they had personally experienced: "What we have heard, what we have seen with our eyes, what we have looked at and touched with our hands, concerning the Word of life" (1 John 1:1). Christianity began as a faith grounded in both historical events and experiential reality—the incarnation, death, and resurrection of Jesus Christ witnessed by His followers.

The Nature of Experiential Evidence

Experiential Apologetics argues that truth must not only be intellectually coherent and evidentially supported but also existentially satisfying. The Christian faith uniquely fulfills humanity's spiritual and moral longings because it corresponds to reality as created by God. Every human being possesses an innate awareness of the divine (Romans 1:19–20) and a conscience that testifies to moral truth (Romans 2:14–15). The universal search for meaning, forgiveness, and hope points to humanity's need for reconciliation with its Creator.

Experiential evidence, then, includes the inward conviction of the Holy Spirit, the moral regeneration of the believer, and the collective witness of the Christian community throughout history. When individuals encounter the truth of the gospel, they experience repentance, peace, and transformation—evidences that cannot be explained by psychological suggestion or social influence alone. Paul's conversion on the road to Damascus (Acts 9:1–6) exemplifies such experiential proof: a zealous persecutor of Christians became the foremost advocate of the faith he once opposed. His life change stands as experiential confirmation of the reality of the risen Christ.

This transformation continues in every true believer. The one who was once alienated from God is reconciled, receiving a new heart and a renewed mind. "If anyone is in Christ, he is a new creation; the old things passed away; behold, new things have come" (2 Corinthians 5:17). Such moral and spiritual renewal provides powerful testimony to the truth of Christianity. The experience of salvation—the forgiveness of sins and the restoration of fellowship with Jehovah—is a living argument that transcends mere intellectual assent.

The Relationship Between Experience and Truth

Experiential Apologetics insists that experience must be tested and interpreted by Scripture. Experience by itself cannot establish truth, for human feelings are fallible and subjective. False religions and mystic philosophies also claim profound experiences, yet these are often deceptive and contradictory. Therefore, experience becomes apologetically valid only when it aligns with the objective truth revealed in the Bible.

The proper relationship between experience and truth is one of confirmation, not foundation. The Word of God stands as the ultimate authority, while experience bears witness to its reality. This mirrors the pattern found in Scripture itself: God reveals truth, and His people experience its power. For example, when Jesus healed the blind, the man could say with certainty, "Though I was blind, now I see" (John 9:25). His experience confirmed the divine authority of Christ's word and work.

The same principle applies to salvation. A believer's assurance rests not upon emotion but upon the truth of God's promises. However, the joy, peace, and transformation that follow genuine faith serve as experiential evidence that those promises are true. Thus, experience is the fruit of truth, not its root.

The Transformative Power of Christianity

One of the most compelling aspects of Experiential Apologetics is the undeniable transformation produced by the gospel in individual lives and entire societies. Christianity changes hearts, restores families, and reforms nations. Wherever the Word of God has been faithfully proclaimed, moral renewal has followed. The abolition of slavery, the establishment of hospitals and schools, and the elevation of human dignity all find their roots in Christian conviction. These effects are experiential evidence that Christianity is divinely empowered.

The early church's explosive growth cannot be explained merely by social or political factors. It grew because people encountered the risen Christ through the preaching of the apostles and the witness of transformed lives. The book of Acts records that multitudes believed as they observed the believers' courage, unity, and moral purity (Acts 2:42–47; 4:13–20). The transformation of the apostles—from fearful deserters to bold proclaimers of the gospel—stands as a living testimony that they had truly encountered the resurrected Lord.

Throughout history, men and women have been radically changed by Christ. Augustine, John Newton, William Wilberforce, and countless others experienced inner transformation that reason and morality alone could not produce. Their lives, marked by repentance, humility, and love for God, testify that Christianity is more than an ideology—it is the living power of God unto salvation.

The Witness of the Holy Spirit

Central to Experiential Apologetics is the inward witness of the Holy Spirit. While the Spirit does not indwell believers in the miraculous sense as some claim, He operates through the Word to convict, illuminate, and assure. This inward conviction is experiential evidence that confirms the truth of Scripture to the heart of the believer.

Jesus promised that the Spirit would testify to the truth: "When the Helper comes, whom I will send to you from the Father, the Spirit of truth who proceeds from the Father, He will bear witness about Me" (John 15:26). The Spirit bears witness through the inspired Word, enabling believers to perceive its divine origin and power. The Word of God, when read or heard, produces conviction and transformation that testify to its divine source (Hebrews 4:12).

This witness is not mystical emotion but rational assurance grounded in God's revelation. It is the Spirit's confirmation that what Scripture declares is indeed reality. The believer knows the truth experientially because the truth has taken hold of his heart. Such internal testimony, combined with the external evidence of Scripture and history, forms a comprehensive apologetic defense.

The Limitations of Experience

Experiential Apologetics, though powerful, must be applied carefully. Experience is always secondary to revelation. The danger arises when feelings or subjective impressions are elevated above Scripture. Many false movements—mysticism, charismatic emotionalism, or universalism—claim authority through experience divorced from biblical truth. Such errors illustrate the need to test all experiences against the Word of God (1 John 4:1).

Christian experience must be doctrinally sound. The true work of God's Spirit always aligns with Scripture and leads to obedience, humility, and holiness. Any experience that contradicts the revealed Word or promotes self-glorification is false. The classical and biblical approach to apologetics ensures that experience is properly interpreted within the framework of objective truth.

Furthermore, personal experience alone cannot persuade the skeptic. While testimony to transformed lives is compelling, it must be accompanied by the rational and historical evidence of Christianity's truth. Experiential Apologetics works most effectively in conjunction with other approaches, confirming what reason and revelation have already established.

The Experiential Testimony of the Church

The collective experience of the body of Christ across centuries provides further validation of Christianity's truth. The Church, composed of believers from every nation and background, stands as a living witness to the power of the gospel. Despite persecution, division, and hardship, it endures and continues to spread because it is founded upon divine truth. Jesus promised, "I will build My church, and the gates of Hades will not overpower it" (Matthew 16:18). The fulfillment of this promise throughout history is experiential proof of God's sustaining power.

The endurance of Christian faith under persecution also testifies to its experiential reality. From the martyrs of the early centuries to believers suffering in modern times, countless Christians have faced death with peace and assurance, confident in the truth of their faith. Such unwavering conviction cannot be explained apart from the experiential reality of God's presence and promises.

The Evangelistic Use of Experiential Apologetics

In evangelism, Experiential Apologetics serves as a bridge between the unbeliever's felt needs and the objective truth of the gospel. Many people today are not persuaded by abstract reasoning alone but are moved by authentic testimony of changed lives. When believers share how God has delivered them from sin, healed their brokenness, and given them new purpose, they provide experiential evidence that Christianity works because it is true.

The Samaritan woman at the well provides a biblical example. After encountering Jesus, she testified to her community, "Come, see a man who told me all the things that I have done; is this not the Christ?" (John 4:29). Her personal experience led others to investigate and ultimately to believe for themselves (John 4:42). Thus, experiential testimony often opens the door for intellectual and spiritual conviction.

The Integration of Experience, Reason, and Revelation

The most effective apologetic approach integrates experience, reason, and revelation. Each validates and complements the others. Reason establishes the coherence of truth; revelation provides the content of truth; and experience confirms the reality of truth. Classical and Evidential Apologetics show that Christianity is logically and historically true, while Experiential Apologetics demonstrates that it is existentially and spiritually true.

This holistic defense reflects the totality of God's revelation. Jehovah does not appeal only to the intellect but to the whole person—mind, heart, and will. True faith involves all three: understanding the truth, believing it, and experiencing its transforming power. Thus, Experiential Apologetics is indispensable because it completes the circle of Christian defense. It shows that Christianity is not merely credible in theory but verifiable in life.

Ultimately, Experiential Apologetics points to the reality that the God of Scripture is living and active, still changing lives today. Every redeemed life is a testimony that the gospel is the power of God for salvation (Romans 1:16). This living evidence continues to confirm that the Bible's message is not mythology but reality—truth that can be known, believed, and experienced.

APOLOGETICS 6 What Is Presuppositional Apologetics?

Presuppositional Apologetics begins with the recognition that every worldview is built upon foundational assumptions—presuppositions—that govern how one interprets reality, truth, knowledge, and morality. It asserts that all reasoning, evidence, and interpretation of facts rest upon ultimate commitments that cannot themselves be proven by neutral logic, but rather must be accepted as first principles. For the Christian, those presuppositions are grounded in the truth of divine revelation— specifically, the inspired, inerrant, and infallible Word of God. Therefore, Presuppositional Apologetics does not attempt to prove Christianity from a supposed position of neutrality, for neutrality itself is a myth. Instead, it begins with the self-attesting truth of Scripture and demonstrates that only the biblical worldview provides the necessary preconditions for rational thought, moral order, and coherent existence.

This method defends Christianity by showing the **impossibility of the contrary**—that is, that all non-Christian worldviews, when examined according to their own assumptions, collapse into irrationality and self-contradiction. While other forms of apologetics often argue *toward* theism or Christianity from shared evidential grounds, Presuppositional Apologetics argues *from* Christianity as the only basis upon which reason, evidence, and meaning are intelligible.

The Philosophical Foundation of Presuppositionalism

Presuppositional Apologetics rests upon a profoundly biblical epistemology. The starting point is that God exists and has spoken authoritatively through His Word. Knowledge is possible only because Jehovah, the Creator, has made human reason and reality correspond to each other in a rational and orderly way. Humanity is capable of knowing truth precisely because man is created in the image of God (Genesis 1:26–27). Therefore, all human understanding is dependent upon divine revelation.

The apostle Paul articulates this principle in Colossians 2:3, declaring that in Christ "are hidden all the treasures of wisdom and knowledge." All truth ultimately finds its source in Him. To attempt knowledge apart from God is to sever oneself from the very foundation of knowledge itself. Paul warns believers in Colossians 2:8, "See to it that no one takes you captive through philosophy and empty deception, according to the tradition of men, according to the elementary principles of the world, rather than according to Christ."

Human reason, though created by God, is corrupted by sin. Thus, apart from divine revelation, the fallen mind distorts truth (Romans 1:21–22). This means that unbelieving worldviews are not merely incomplete; they are fundamentally self-defeating because they suppress the knowledge of God that is inherently known through creation and conscience (Romans 1:18–20). The presuppositional apologist therefore begins with the truth of Scripture as the foundation for all reasoning, showing that without the biblical God, the very act of rational thought becomes impossible.

The Myth of Neutrality

One of the defining principles of Presuppositional Apologetics is the rejection of neutrality. The unbeliever often demands that the Christian "set aside faith" and meet on neutral ground to examine evidence. However, Scripture declares that no such neutrality exists. All people interpret evidence through their worldview presuppositions. The unbeliever interprets reality through the lens of rebellion against God, while the believer interprets reality through submission to God's revelation.

Proverbs 1:7 declares, "The fear of Jehovah is the beginning of knowledge." This statement eliminates any claim to autonomous human reasoning. True knowledge begins not with human independence but with reverence toward God. When man attempts to reason apart from his Creator, he is left in intellectual darkness. Psalm 14:1 describes this condition: "The fool has said in his heart, 'There is no God.'" The fool, in biblical terminology, is not intellectually deficient but morally rebellious—rejecting the foundation upon which all knowledge rests.

Presuppositional Apologetics therefore challenges the unbeliever's very starting point rather than conceding it. It does not grant the assumption that human reason alone is a sufficient standard for truth. Instead, it exposes that without the biblical God, the unbeliever has no rational basis for reason, morality, science, or meaning. Every human thought presupposes the order, logic, and moral structure that only the God of Scripture provides.

The Biblical Foundation for Presuppositional Reasoning

Presuppositional Apologetics is deeply rooted in the biblical understanding of human knowledge, sin, and revelation. In Romans 1:18–23, Paul explains that all people know God through the things He has made but suppress that truth in unrighteousness. Their thinking becomes futile because they refuse to honor Him as God. This suppression of truth is not intellectual ignorance but willful rebellion. The result is that unbelievers construct false worldviews that cannot coherently account for the realities they take for granted.

The same principle appears in Proverbs 26:4–5, which encapsulates the presuppositional method: "Do not answer a fool according to his folly, lest you also be like him. Answer a fool according to his folly, lest he be wise in his own eyes." The apologist must not adopt the unbeliever's false presuppositions (v. 4), yet he must expose their folly by demonstrating the absurdity of their worldview when taken to its logical conclusion (v. 5). This twofold method—refusing to reason from unbelief while revealing its incoherence—is the essence of presuppositional defense.

Furthermore, 2 Corinthians 10:4–5 declares that believers are to "destroy speculations and every lofty thing raised up against the knowledge of God, and take every thought captive to the obedience of Christ." Presuppositional Apologetics fulfills this command by showing that all intellectual rebellion against God is irrational and self-destructive, while submission to His revelation restores coherence and understanding.

The Impossibility of the Contrary

At the core of Presuppositional Apologetics lies the principle known as the "impossibility of the contrary." This means that without the biblical worldview, it is impossible to make sense of anything at all. Logic, morality, science, and rational discourse all presuppose a consistent, ordered universe governed by unchanging laws and grounded in objective truth—conditions that only the existence of an eternal, rational, moral Creator can provide.

Unbelievers use logic, reason, and morality daily, yet they cannot justify these concepts within their own worldviews. A materialist worldview cannot explain the existence of immaterial laws of logic. A relativist worldview cannot explain universal moral obligation. A naturalist worldview cannot explain the consistent uniformity of nature upon which science depends. These realities make sense only if the universe was created by a personal, consistent, and rational God who upholds it by His power (Hebrews 1:3). Thus, when the unbeliever argues against God, he must borrow the very principles of rationality and morality that can only exist if God does.

This approach is not a mere philosophical trick but a reflection of biblical truth. Every act of reasoning already assumes the reality of the God who gives order and meaning to thought. The apologist's task is to reveal this dependency to the unbeliever, demonstrating that his worldview collapses under its own weight without the foundation of divine revelation.

The Role of Revelation and the Word of God

In Presuppositional Apologetics, Scripture is not merely one source of evidence among others—it is the ultimate standard by which all truth claims are judged. The Bible is self-authenticating because it bears the marks of divine authority and coherence. The believer does not judge the Word of God by human reasoning; rather, human reasoning must be judged by the Word of God.

Psalm 36:9 declares, "In Your light we see light." This verse expresses the essence of presuppositional thought: we can see and understand anything only by the light of God's revelation. The Bible reveals the world as it truly is, explaining creation, the fall, redemption, and the moral order. Without Scripture, man's understanding remains darkened, fragmented, and ultimately meaningless.

This is why Presuppositional Apologetics maintains that all evidences for Christianity—historical, scientific, or moral—must be interpreted within the framework of biblical revelation. Evidence is never "neutral"; it is always seen through a worldview lens. Only by starting with God's revelation can evidence be properly understood.

The Antithesis Between the Christian and Non-Christian Worldviews

A key concept in Presuppositional Apologetics is the "antithesis" between the Christian and non-Christian worldviews. This antithesis is absolute in principle, though not always in practice, because all truth belongs to God, and even unbelievers, as image-bearers, live within God's created order. They cannot escape His reality, even while denying it.

This tension explains why unbelievers can discover truths in science, mathematics, and ethics—they live in God's world and must operate according to His order to function meaningfully. However, their success in using reason or morality is inconsistent with their professed worldview. Presuppositional Apologetics exposes this inconsistency by showing that only the biblical worldview provides the necessary foundation for these activities.

For example, the atheist who insists on moral outrage at injustice must borrow moral standards from the Christian worldview. If humanity is merely the product of chance and evolution, moral obligation has no foundation. Yet atheists cannot live as though moral relativism were true; their behavior and conscience testify to their dependence upon God's moral law written on the heart (Romans 2:14–15).

The Method of Presuppositional Engagement

The presuppositional method of engagement involves three essential steps: **identification, internal critique, and gospel presentation**.

First, the apologist identifies the unbeliever's presuppositions—the foundational assumptions underlying his worldview. Second, he performs an internal critique, showing that the unbeliever's worldview cannot provide the preconditions for logic, knowledge, or morality. This exposes the irrationality of unbelief. Finally, the apologist presents the Christian worldview, demonstrating that it alone provides the foundation for rational thought, moral truth, and human dignity.

This method does not abandon evidence or reason but places them in their proper context—under the authority of Scripture. The goal is not to "prove" God to those who demand empirical neutrality but to demonstrate that apart from God, nothing can be proved or known at all.

The Practical Power of Presuppositional Apologetics

Presuppositional Apologetics equips believers to confront the intellectual and moral chaos of modern culture. In an age of relativism and skepticism, it restores confidence in the absolute authority of God's Word. It reminds Christians that they need not adopt worldly assumptions to defend their faith; rather, they can stand firmly on the revealed truth of Scripture.

This approach also strengthens personal faith. The believer who understands that all truth depends on God's revelation sees that Christianity is not merely one option among many but the foundation of all reality. Every fact, every law, every truth points back to the Creator who sustains all things. Presuppositional reasoning turns apologetics from defensive reaction to confident proclamation: the world only makes sense because Jehovah reigns.

Moreover, this method exalts God rather than human intellect. It honors Him as the ultimate authority in every area of thought and life. When believers defend the faith presuppositionally, they are not appealing to human autonomy but declaring that "the sum of Your word is truth" (Psalm 119:160). They demonstrate that all wisdom begins and ends in God, and that the fear of Jehovah is the only true foundation of knowledge.

The Integration of Presuppositional and Classical Approaches

Although Presuppositional Apologetics differs from Classical and Evidential approaches in method, it does not oppose them in purpose. Each approach contributes to the unified defense of truth. The classical apologist shows that theism is reasonable; the evidential apologist presents historical and empirical support for Christianity; the presuppositional apologist reveals that all reasoning itself depends on God. Together, they form a comprehensive apologetic that addresses the unbeliever's mind, heart, and conscience.

Presuppositional Apologetics, however, provides the necessary foundation for all other methods. It ensures that the defense of the faith remains rooted in divine revelation rather than human autonomy. The apologist who begins with Scripture can confidently use evidence and reason, knowing that their validity depends on the God who authored both.

Conclusion: The Lordship of Christ Over All Thought

Presuppositional Apologetics proclaims that Christ's Lordship extends not only over the church but over all knowledge, logic, and existence. Every thought must be brought into obedience to Him. The believer's task is to expose the futility of unbelief and to declare that true wisdom, reason, and morality are possible only through submission to the revealed Word of God.

Christianity does not need to be proven by external standards of truth—it is itself the standard by which all truth is measured. The apologist's confidence rests not in persuasive eloquence but in the unshakable authority of Scripture. The Word of God is the light in which all knowledge is seen, the foundation upon which all truth stands, and the revelation through which Jehovah makes Himself known.

Thus, Presuppositional Apologetics calls every person to abandon autonomy and acknowledge that "the fear of Jehovah is the beginning of wisdom" (Proverbs 9:10). In doing so, it vindicates the supremacy of God's truth and demonstrates that all other foundations are sinking sand.

APOLOGETICS 7 Reaching Hearts with the Art of Persuasion

Christian Apologetics is not merely the intellectual defense of the faith; it is also the spiritual art of persuasion—reaching both the minds and hearts of those who do not yet know the truth. While reason, logic, and evidence are essential, they serve a higher purpose: to bring people into a right relationship with Jehovah through Jesus Christ. True apologetics seeks not only to refute falsehood but to restore the image of God in fallen humanity through the power of divine truth. This work of persuasion reflects the heart of the gospel itself, for Christianity is not a cold system of propositions but the living truth that transforms souls.

The effective apologist must understand that persuasion is more than argumentation. It involves compassion, patience, and spiritual wisdom. Persuasion is the bridge between truth and transformation—the means by which eternal realities are made understandable, believable, and compelling to the human heart. Every apologist is called to be both a defender and a persuader: one who reasons clearly and loves deeply, reflecting the character of Christ in both conviction and gentleness.

The Biblical Foundation for Persuasion

Throughout Scripture, persuasion is central to the proclamation of truth. The term *peithō*, translated "persuade," appears repeatedly in the New Testament to describe the method of apostolic preaching. Paul wrote, "Therefore, knowing the fear of the Lord, we persuade men" (2 Corinthians 5:11). His motivation was not pride in argument but reverence for God and compassion for those destined for judgment.

Paul's ministry demonstrates that apologetics and evangelism are inseparable acts of persuasion. He reasoned in synagogues, marketplaces, and before rulers, not merely to win debates but to lead people to faith in Christ. Acts 17:2–4 records that he "reasoned with them from the Scriptures, explaining and giving evidence that the Christ had to suffer and rise again from the dead." The result was that "some of them were persuaded." In Acts 26:28, even King Agrippa confessed, "In a short time you are persuading me to become a Christian."

Jesus Himself embodied divine persuasion. His words carried moral authority and spiritual conviction. When He spoke, hearts were pierced (Luke 24:32). His teaching appealed to both reason and conscience, exposing falsehood and inviting repentance. His miracles confirmed His message, and His compassion drew sinners to the truth. Jesus demonstrated that persuasion flows not from manipulation but from divine authenticity—the harmony of truth spoken in love.

The Nature of True Persuasion

Persuasion in the Christian sense differs profoundly from worldly rhetoric or manipulation. Secular persuasion seeks to influence others for personal or political gain, often appealing to emotion without truth. Biblical persuasion, by contrast, appeals to the whole person—mind, conscience, and will—through truth communicated in love. It respects human freedom and the dignity of the listener while calling for a response to God's revealed truth.

True persuasion is built upon integrity and humility. The apologist must never coerce or humiliate an unbeliever but must reason honestly and speak with compassion. Persuasion is effective only when the speaker's life aligns with his message. Paul could confidently exhort others to imitate him as he imitated Christ (1 Corinthians 11:1) because his message and character were consistent. The most eloquent arguments lose power when the life behind them lacks sincerity.

Persuasion also requires understanding the human heart. People resist truth not merely because of intellectual misunderstanding but because of spiritual blindness and moral rebellion. The apologist must recognize this and approach others with both firmness and grace. Persuasion seeks not only to convince the mind but to confront the conscience. It calls the hearer to repentance, offering the hope of forgiveness and reconciliation through Christ.

The Role of the Holy Spirit in Persuasion

No amount of eloquence, logic, or human effort can bring spiritual conviction apart from the work of the Holy Spirit. Jesus declared that the Spirit "will convict the world concerning sin and righteousness and judgment" (John 16:8). The apologist is an instrument in God's hand, but the Spirit alone opens the heart. This truth protects the apologist from pride and discouragement. Success in persuasion does not depend on human skill but on divine empowerment through the Word.

The Spirit operates through truth, not apart from it. When believers faithfully proclaim the Word of God, the Spirit uses that truth to awaken the conscience and draw sinners to Christ. Hebrews 4:12 describes the Word as "living and active and sharper than any two-edged sword." The apologist's task, therefore, is not to invent persuasive methods but to present the truth clearly, allowing the Spirit to do the work of transformation.

This cooperation between divine power and human faithfulness illustrates that persuasion is both an art and a ministry. The apologist prepares intellectually and spiritually, yet prays that God will accomplish what only He can do—change hearts.

Persuasion and the Power of Character

Persuasion flows as much from who the apologist is as from what he says. A life marked by holiness, humility, and compassion gives weight to every argument. The messenger's credibility becomes part of the message. The Apostle Paul's persuasion was effective not merely because of his reasoning but because of his integrity and endurance. He wrote, "Our exhortation does not come from error or impurity or by way of deceit; but just as we have been approved by God to be entrusted with the gospel, so we speak, not as pleasing men, but God who examines our hearts" (1 Thessalonians 2:3–4).

A persuasive apologist must cultivate spiritual maturity. Pride, harshness, or self-righteousness destroy persuasion. The servant of God must demonstrate the fruits of the Spirit—love, patience, kindness, and self-control (Galatians 5:22–23). A spirit of gentleness often accomplishes more than the most brilliant reasoning. Proverbs 16:21 affirms, "The wise in heart will be called understanding, and sweetness of speech increases persuasiveness."

Persuasion is most powerful when it springs from love. Jesus' compassion for sinners moved Him to speak truth even when it offended. He wept over Jerusalem's unbelief (Luke 19:41–42). The apologist who weeps for the lost will speak with a tenderness that mere argument can never produce. The world is not converted by intellectual might but by truth expressed through sacrificial love.

Understanding the Barriers to Belief

Effective persuasion requires discernment. The apologist must understand the intellectual and emotional barriers that keep people from accepting truth. Some reject Christianity because of moral rebellion—they do not want to submit to divine authority. Others struggle with doubt due to personal pain, hypocrisy in the church, or misunderstanding of Scripture. Persuasion involves addressing both the reasons and the motivations behind unbelief.

To the proud skeptic, persuasion must expose the futility of autonomy and the self-contradiction of unbelief. To the wounded seeker, persuasion must offer compassion and hope. Jesus modeled this balance perfectly: He confronted the Pharisees' pride with truth, yet comforted the brokenhearted with mercy. The apologist must likewise discern when to reason sharply and when to speak softly. "A word spoken in right circumstances is like apples of gold in settings of silver" (Proverbs 25:11).

Persuasion also involves patience. Conversion rarely happens instantly. Paul "reasoned daily" in the hall of Tyrannus (Acts 19:9), showing persistence in dialogue. The apologist must be willing to invest time, build trust, and allow God to work gradually in the listener's heart.

The Harmony of Logic and Love

Christian persuasion unites logic with love. Logic presents the truth clearly; love opens the heart to receive it. Without logic, faith is groundless; without love, truth is lifeless. The harmony of these two elements reflects the nature of Christ Himself, who is both "full of grace and truth" (John 1:14).

Logic alone may convince the intellect, but love wins the person. The apologist who wields truth without compassion may silence opposition but will not change hearts. Likewise, love without truth leads only to sentimentality. The persuasive apologist must therefore speak truth in love (Ephesians 4:15), demonstrating that the gospel addresses both the mind's questions and the heart's longings.

This balance guards against extremes. Overemphasis on intellect can produce cold argumentation, while emotionalism can lead to shallow faith. The apologist's task is to communicate the unchanging truth of Scripture in a way that satisfies reason and awakens devotion.

Persuasion and the Use of Testimony

Personal testimony is a powerful tool in persuasion. While facts and arguments establish the credibility of Christianity, testimony demonstrates its reality. When believers share how the gospel has changed their lives—bringing forgiveness, peace, and purpose—they provide experiential evidence that complements rational defense.

Paul frequently used his own testimony as part of his apologetic. Before Agrippa, he recounted his conversion from persecutor to preacher (Acts 26:9–23). His story combined logic with personal experience, illustrating that the truth of Christ transforms life itself. Likewise, every believer possesses a testimony that can reach others. The apologist's life becomes a living argument for the power of God's grace.

Testimony, however, must always point to Scripture and Christ, not self. The goal is not to glorify experience but to glorify the Savior who redeems. When personal testimony is coupled with biblical truth, it becomes a persuasive witness that God's Word is both true and alive.

The Persuasive Use of Questions

One of the most effective methods of persuasion in Scripture and practice is the use of questions. Jesus often persuaded by asking questions that exposed false assumptions and invited reflection. "Who do you say that I am?" (Matthew 16:15) compelled His disciples to confront the truth personally. Questions engage the listener's mind and conscience, leading them to discover truth for themselves.

The apologist who learns to ask wise and probing questions disarms hostility and encourages honest dialogue. Questions uncover presuppositions, reveal inconsistencies, and invite deeper thought. They turn confrontation into conversation, helping the unbeliever reason toward truth rather than feel cornered by it. This Socratic approach, modeled by Christ Himself, remains one of the most persuasive tools in evangelism and apologetics.

Persuasion as a Reflection of God's Character

The art of persuasion reflects the character of Jehovah Himself, who reasons with humanity rather than coercing it. "Come now, and let us reason together," He invites, "Though your sins are as scarlet, they will be as white as snow" (Isaiah 1:18). God appeals to reason and conscience, inviting repentance through truth and mercy.

Throughout Scripture, divine persuasion is evident. God persuaded Noah to build the ark through His Word of warning, persuaded Abraham to trust His promises, and persuaded Israel through miracles and covenant. The prophets pleaded with the people to return to Jehovah. Jesus persuaded His followers by revealing truth in word and deed, never forcing belief but calling for voluntary faith.

Thus, persuasion is not merely a rhetorical skill; it is a divine attribute expressed through human ministry. When believers persuade others toward truth, they participate in God's redemptive mission.

The End of Persuasion: The Glory of God

The ultimate goal of persuasion is not intellectual victory or emotional satisfaction but the glory of God through the salvation of souls. When an unbeliever is persuaded to embrace the truth, it is God who receives the honor. The apologist must therefore labor faithfully, trusting the results to Him. "I planted, Apollos watered, but God was causing the growth" (1 Corinthians 3:6).

Reaching hearts with the art of persuasion requires prayer as much as preparation, humility as much as boldness, and truth as much as tenderness. The persuasive Christian is one who mirrors the heart of Christ—speaking truth uncompromisingly yet with compassion that draws rather than drives away.

In the end, the art of persuasion is the art of love in truth. It is the means by which the eternal Word reaches human hearts, transforming disbelief into faith, rebellion into worship, and darkness into light. The apologist who masters this divine art becomes a true ambassador of Christ, whose words and life together testify that the truth of Jehovah is not only credible but irresistible.

Edward D. Andrews

APOLOGETICS 8
Developing the Art of Effective Evangelism

Evangelism is the divinely ordained means by which the message of salvation is proclaimed to a lost world. It is the heartbeat of the Christian faith and the fulfillment of Christ's command to "go therefore and make disciples of all the nations" (Matthew 28:19). Yet, true evangelism is not a mechanical act or a formulaic approach; it is an art—a Spirit-guided expression of truth communicated through love, wisdom, and conviction. Developing the art of effective evangelism involves understanding the message, mastering the method, embodying the message through one's life, and relying upon the power of God's Word to transform hearts.

The Christian evangelist is not a salesman seeking to win converts through persuasion alone but a servant of Christ proclaiming the truth of salvation through His Word. The responsibility of the believer is to sow the seed faithfully; the power to bring new life rests with Jehovah alone. As Paul affirmed, "I planted, Apollos watered, but God was causing the growth" (1 Corinthians 3:6). This principle defines all effective evangelism—it is God-centered, Word-driven, and Spirit-empowered.

The Biblical Foundation of Evangelism

The call to evangelism is not optional but essential to the Christian life. Jesus declared, "You shall be My witnesses both in Jerusalem, and in all Judea and Samaria, and even to the end of the earth" (Acts 1:8). The early church understood this as a sacred duty and a joyful privilege. Their witness was not limited to public preaching but extended into homes, marketplaces, and personal relationships. Wherever they went, they spoke of the risen Christ.

Evangelism begins with the conviction that the gospel is true, necessary, and urgent. It proclaims that all humanity is under sin, alienated from God, and destined for destruction apart from repentance and faith in Christ. Romans 3:23 declares, "All have sinned and fall short of the glory of God." Yet, the good news follows: "The wages of sin is death, but the gracious gift of God is eternal life in Christ Jesus our Lord" (Romans 6:23).

Every believer, therefore, becomes an ambassador for Christ, entrusted with the ministry of reconciliation (2 Corinthians 5:18–20). This ministry involves communicating the gospel clearly, accurately, and compassionately so that others may understand and respond in faith.

The Message of Evangelism

The effectiveness of evangelism depends first upon the purity of its message. The gospel is not a general invitation to moral improvement or religious experience—it is the announcement of divine redemption accomplished through the life, death, and resurrection of Jesus Christ. Paul summarized the message succinctly: "That Christ died for our sins according to the Scriptures, and that He was buried, and that He was raised on the third day according to the Scriptures" (1 Corinthians 15:3–4).

This message must never be diluted to please the world. Effective evangelism requires clarity regarding humanity's sin, the necessity of repentance, and the exclusivity of salvation in Christ. Jesus said, "No one comes to the Father except through Me" (John 14:6). To proclaim anything less is to betray the gospel's power. The evangelist must resist the temptation to compromise truth for acceptance, remembering that the gospel is "the power of God for salvation to everyone who believes" (Romans 1:16).

The message also includes the promise of transformation. Those who believe are forgiven, reconciled to God, and given new life. Evangelism, therefore, calls not merely for intellectual assent but for personal surrender to the Lordship of Christ. The gospel changes the heart and renews the mind, producing obedience, hope, and holiness.

The Motivation for Evangelism

Effective evangelism flows from the right motivation—a heart compelled by love for God and compassion for the lost. Paul expressed this passion when he wrote, "Woe is me if I do not preach the gospel!" (1 Corinthians 9:16). The true evangelist is driven not by duty alone but by gratitude for grace. The more one appreciates the depth of personal salvation, the stronger the desire becomes to share it.

Love for Jehovah motivates obedience to His commission. Love for others inspires compassion toward those still in darkness. Jesus' ministry exemplified both. He came "to seek and to save that which was lost" (Luke 19:10), moved by compassion for the crowds who were "distressed and downcast like sheep without a shepherd" (Matthew 9:36). Effective evangelism imitates this heart of Christ—truth spoken in love, motivated by mercy.

Evangelism also flows from conviction. The evangelist must be persuaded that eternal life and death are real, that Christ is the only Savior, and that the time is short. Without this sense of urgency, evangelism becomes perfunctory or neglected. The faithful messenger remembers that each soul will one day stand before the judgment seat of God, making the call to repentance a matter of eternal consequence.

The Method of Evangelism

While the gospel message never changes, the methods of communication must adapt to context and audience. The effective evangelist understands that people come from diverse backgrounds, experiences, and worldviews. Paul demonstrated this flexibility in his ministry. When speaking to Jews, he reasoned from Scripture; when addressing Gentiles, he began with creation and natural revelation (Acts 17:22–31). Though his approach varied, his message remained the same—Christ crucified and risen.

Evangelism takes many forms: public proclamation, personal conversation, written testimony, or compassionate service accompanied by truth. However, all methods share the same goal—to make the message of salvation understandable and convicting. The most effective evangelism occurs through personal relationships, where trust allows truth to penetrate the heart.

The art of evangelism requires careful listening as well as speaking. The evangelist must understand the questions, fears, and objections of others before answering them with Scripture. Proverbs 18:13 warns, "He who gives an answer before he hears, it is folly and shame to him." Listening demonstrates respect and compassion, qualities that open the door for genuine dialogue.

The Role of Apologetics in Evangelism

Evangelism and apologetics are inseparably linked. Apologetics provides the rational foundation that strengthens evangelism by removing intellectual obstacles to faith. Peter's call to defend the faith was not theoretical but evangelistic—Christians are to give "an account for the hope that is in you." Apologetics equips believers to explain *why* the gospel is true and *why* all other worldviews fail to satisfy reason and morality.

In practice, apologetics functions as the pre-evangelistic stage of persuasion. It prepares the soil of the heart by answering objections, clarifying misconceptions, and exposing the insufficiency of unbelief. Yet, apologetics alone cannot convert; it must always lead to proclamation of the gospel. The goal is not to win arguments but to win souls. Reason clears the way, but only the Word and Spirit bring life.

Therefore, the effective evangelist must be both apologist and witness—defending truth intellectually and proclaiming it personally. The two are not separate disciplines but complementary expressions of obedience to Christ.

The Power of Scripture in Evangelism

The central instrument of all evangelism is the Word of God. The Bible alone possesses divine authority and spiritual power to bring conviction, conversion, and transformation. Isaiah 55:11 affirms that God's Word "will not return to Me empty, without accomplishing what I desire." The evangelist must trust this promise, relying not on clever speech or emotional appeal but on the sufficiency of Scripture.

The early church's success in spreading the gospel came from their unwavering confidence in the power of the Word. They did not depend on social influence, wealth, or philosophy. They simply preached Christ crucified and risen, and lives were changed. The same principle holds today. Methods may vary, but the message must remain rooted in the inspired Word.

Quoting and explaining Scripture in evangelism is vital, for faith "comes from hearing, and hearing by the word of Christ" (Romans 10:17). The Word pierces the heart, awakens conscience, and reveals both sin and grace. Every evangelistic encounter should be grounded in Scripture's authority, for it alone speaks with the voice of God.

The Life of the Evangelist

The messenger's life must authenticate the message. Hypocrisy nullifies credibility. The effective evangelist embodies the truth he proclaims, living with integrity, humility, and holiness. Paul urged Timothy to "pay close attention to yourself and to your teaching" (1 Timothy 4:16). A consistent life is the most persuasive argument for the gospel's transforming power.

This does not mean perfection but authenticity. The evangelist must be quick to confess sin and demonstrate the same grace he preaches. The world is not drawn to flawless people but to forgiven ones. A life marked by love, patience, and kindness makes the message attractive. Jesus described believers as "the light of the world" (Matthew 5:14), called to reflect

His character through good works that glorify the Father.

Prayer is likewise essential. The evangelist's effectiveness depends on communion with God. Before speaking to others about Christ, he must speak to Christ about others. The greatest evangelistic victories are born in prayer, for only God can open blind eyes and soften hard hearts.

Overcoming Fear and Indifference

One of the greatest barriers to effective evangelism is fear—the fear of rejection, ridicule, or failure. Yet Scripture commands believers to speak boldly. Paul asked for prayer "that I may open my mouth to make known with boldness the mystery of the gospel" (Ephesians 6:19). Courage does not mean absence of fear but obedience in spite of it. Confidence comes from knowing that the message is true, the mission is divine, and the outcome belongs to God.

Indifference is another barrier. Many believers lack a burden for souls because they have lost sight of eternal realities. To recover passion for evangelism, one must meditate on the reality of judgment, the love of Christ, and the urgency of time. Every person encountered is an eternal being whose destiny depends on their response to the gospel. Recognizing this truth reignites compassion and compels action.

Cultural Discernment in Evangelism

Effective evangelism also requires cultural discernment. The evangelist must understand the society in which he lives—its philosophies, idols, and moral assumptions—so he can communicate truth clearly. Paul's address at Mars Hill (Acts 17) exemplifies this. He began by observing the Athenians' altar "to an unknown god" and used it as a bridge to proclaim the true God. Likewise, Christians today must engage culture with discernment, identifying points of contact while refusing to compromise biblical truth.

Cultural relevance does not mean conformity. The gospel transcends culture, confronting sin while offering redemption. The evangelist must speak in language the hearer understands but remain faithful to Scripture's unchanging message. The goal is not to make Christianity acceptable but to make it understandable.

The Goal of Evangelism: Discipleship

The aim of evangelism is not merely conversion but discipleship. Jesus commanded believers to "make disciples," not simply to count converts. Genuine evangelism continues after the initial response, guiding new believers into growth, obedience, and maturity. The Great Commission includes both proclamation and instruction—"teaching them to observe all that I commanded you" (Matthew 28:20).

Effective evangelism therefore requires follow-up, mentorship, and integration into the community of faith. The local church becomes the nurturing ground for spiritual growth. Without discipleship, evangelism becomes incomplete; without evangelism, discipleship never begins. Both belong to the same divine mission.

The Eternal Perspective of Evangelism

Evangelism is ultimately about eternity. Every act of witness participates in God's plan to redeem people from every tribe and tongue. Revelation 7:9 gives a glimpse of the outcome—a great multitude standing before the throne, redeemed by the blood of the Lamb. The evangelist labors with this vision in mind, knowing that his work contributes to the fulfillment of God's eternal purpose.

Faithfulness in evangelism is never wasted. Even when results are unseen, God's Word accomplishes His purpose. The evangelist may sow in tears, but he will reap in joy (Psalm 126:5). This eternal perspective sustains perseverance, assuring that every effort made for the gospel echoes forever.

Conclusion: Evangelism as Worship

Evangelism is an act of worship. It is the overflow of a heart that treasures Christ above all and desires others to share in that joy. The effective evangelist proclaims not out of obligation but out of adoration. His message is not merely "You must believe," but "Behold the glory of the Savior who alone is worthy of belief."

To develop the art of effective evangelism is to cultivate a life that reflects Christ, speaks His truth with clarity, and loves souls with His compassion. It is to let the light of the gospel shine through every word and deed so that others may glorify God. Evangelism is not simply a task to be done; it is a way of life that flows from knowing the living God and desiring His glory among the nations.

APOLOGETICS 9 Imitate Jesus When Evangelizing

Jesus Christ is the perfect example of how to communicate the truth of God to humanity. His entire ministry embodied divine wisdom, love, and compassion united with unwavering devotion to truth. Every word He spoke, every act He performed, and every encounter He had with individuals reflected the heart and character of Jehovah. To imitate Jesus when evangelizing is to follow the pattern of the Master Evangelist, the One who came "to seek and to save that which was lost" (Luke 19:10).

The art of evangelism is not learned merely through strategy or technique; it is learned through imitation—by studying how Jesus reached people and by conforming our attitude, approach, and message to His. Evangelism that reflects Christ must therefore be faithful to His truth, filled with His compassion, and guided by His example.

The Model of Christ's Evangelism

Jesus' ministry was marked by perfect balance— He was both compassionate and confrontational, gentle yet firm, personal yet purposeful. He did not adapt truth to please His audience, but He adapted His approach to reach their hearts. Every encounter was intentional and tailored to the spiritual condition of the hearer. His method flowed from His nature, and His nature was divine truth expressed in love.

From the beginning of His ministry, Jesus proclaimed the gospel message with clarity and authority: "Repent, for the kingdom of heaven is at hand" (Matthew 4:17). He never softened the necessity of repentance, yet He offered forgiveness and grace to all who turned to God. His message combined moral urgency with merciful invitation. To imitate Jesus in evangelism is to maintain this same balance—proclaiming repentance and faith in God's grace without compromise.

Jesus' Compassion for the Lost

The foundation of Jesus' evangelism was compassion. He saw people not as adversaries or statistics but as souls in need of salvation. Matthew 9:36 records that "seeing the crowds, He felt compassion for them, because they were distressed and downcast like sheep without a shepherd." His heart ached for their spiritual blindness and suffering.

True evangelism begins with the same spirit of compassion. The effective evangelist must see beyond outward rebellion or indifference to the inner condition of the heart. Every person without Christ is spiritually lost, enslaved to sin, and alienated from Jehovah. Compassion drives the believer to speak, not out of pride or obligation, but out of love that seeks to rescue others from destruction.

Jesus' compassion was not passive emotion but active mercy. He fed the hungry, healed the sick, and comforted the broken—all as expressions of divine love that opened hearts to receive truth. The believer who imitates Christ will likewise demonstrate the gospel through deeds of kindness and concern, allowing actions to prepare the way for words.

Jesus' Use of Scripture

Jesus' authority in evangelism came from His reliance upon Scripture. Throughout His ministry, He consistently appealed to the written Word as the ultimate standard of truth. When confronting temptation in the wilderness, He defeated Satan's lies by declaring, "It is written" (Matthew 4:4, 7, 10). When teaching or correcting others, He grounded His message in Scripture's authority, affirming that "Scripture cannot be broken" (John 10:35).

Imitating Jesus means evangelizing with the same confidence in the power of God's Word. The evangelist must never rely on personal opinion, emotional appeal, or worldly wisdom but on the timeless truth of Scripture. It is the Word that convicts the conscience, exposes sin, and reveals the Savior. Hebrews 4:12 affirms that "the word of God is living and active and sharper than any two-edged sword."

The evangelist who faithfully uses Scripture in conversation allows God Himself to speak. Jesus' example shows that the power of evangelism lies not in the eloquence of the messenger but in the authority of the message.

Jesus' Personal Engagement

Jesus was masterful in personal encounters. He met people where they were, addressing their specific needs, doubts, and misconceptions. Each conversation was intimate, purposeful, and transformative.

His interaction with the Samaritan woman at the well (John 4:4–26) demonstrates this beautifully. Jesus began with a simple request for water, bridging cultural barriers to establish dialogue. He then exposed her spiritual thirst, leading her to recognize her sin and need for the Messiah. His approach combined patience, wisdom, and compassion, resulting in her conversion and subsequent witness to others.

Similarly, when speaking with Nicodemus (John 3:1–21), a respected Pharisee, Jesus adapted His approach. He spoke intellectually and spiritually, challenging Nicodemus's reliance on religious tradition by declaring, "You must be born again." Jesus always led conversations toward spiritual truth, never leaving individuals with mere curiosity but pressing them toward decision.

To imitate Jesus, believers must learn to engage people personally, discerning their spiritual condition and guiding them gently but firmly toward truth. Evangelism is most effective when it moves from abstract proclamation to personal interaction.

Jesus' Boldness and Clarity

Jesus never compromised the truth to avoid conflict or offense. Though gentle in demeanor, He spoke with divine authority and clarity. He confronted sin directly, exposing hypocrisy and error without apology. His boldness stemmed from His complete confidence in the Father's will and His commitment to truth.

In John 8:24, Jesus declared, "Unless you believe that I am He, you will die in your sins." Such words cut through false religion and moral pretense, forcing listeners to face the reality of their need for salvation. Yet even in confrontation, His purpose was redemptive—to awaken repentance, not to condemn unjustly.

Believers must learn from this example. The modern tendency to soften biblical truth in the name of tolerance betrays the gospel's power. The imitation of Christ requires courage to speak truth even when it offends worldly sensibilities. However, that courage must always be tempered with grace, ensuring that firmness never becomes harshness. Truth and love must remain inseparable.

Jesus' Dependence on Prayer

Prayer was central to Jesus' ministry and essential to His evangelism. He sought the Father's guidance before major decisions, withdrew to pray after periods of ministry, and interceded for those He came to save. Luke 5:16 notes that "Jesus Himself would often slip away to the wilderness and pray." His communion with the Father sustained His mission and directed His words.

If the Son of God relied upon prayer in His ministry, how much more must His followers do the same? Evangelism without prayer is powerless, for it depends upon human effort rather than divine strength. Prayer prepares the evangelist's heart, softens the hearts of listeners, and invites the Holy Spirit to work through the Word. The one who imitates Jesus will make prayer the foundation of all outreach—seeking wisdom, boldness, and compassion through continual dependence upon God.

Jesus' Focus on the Kingdom

Jesus' evangelism always pointed toward the Kingdom of God. His message was not merely about personal forgiveness but about submission to divine rule. He proclaimed, "The time is fulfilled, and the kingdom of God is at hand; repent and believe in the gospel" (Mark 1:15).

This kingdom focus reminds believers that evangelism is not about personal success, social reform, or emotional experience—it is about calling people to acknowledge Jehovah's sovereignty and enter His eternal reign through Christ. The evangelist who imitates Jesus will maintain this eternal perspective, proclaiming not a human-centered gospel but a God-centered one.

Jesus never flattered His listeners with promises of worldly ease; instead, He called them to self-denial and discipleship: "If anyone wishes to come after Me, he must deny himself, and take up his cross and follow Me" (Matthew 16:24). Imitating Him means presenting the cost of discipleship honestly while emphasizing the incomparable reward of knowing and serving the living God.

Jesus' Perseverance Amid Rejection

Even the perfect Evangelist faced rejection. Many heard His words but refused to believe. John 1:11 declares, "He came to His own, and those who were His own did not receive Him." Yet Jesus never allowed rejection to hinder His mission. He continued preaching, teaching, and healing, fully obedient to the Father's plan.

Evangelists must expect the same. Faithfulness, not visible success, defines effective evangelism. The servant is not greater than his Master; if Jesus faced rejection, His followers will too. However, perseverance in witness reflects the love and patience of Christ. Even when hearts seem hardened, the evangelist must continue sowing the seed, trusting that God will bring fruit in His time.

Jesus demonstrated this patience on the cross, praying for His persecutors, "Father, forgive them; for they do not know what they are doing" (Luke 23:34). Such grace toward unbelief is the ultimate model for all who proclaim the gospel.

Jesus' Empowerment of His Followers

Before ascending to heaven, Jesus entrusted His mission to His disciples, empowering them through the Holy Spirit. He said, "You will receive power when the Holy Spirit has come upon you; and you shall be My witnesses" (Acts 1:8). The same Spirit who empowered Christ's ministry empowers believers today through the Word of God.

Imitating Jesus means evangelizing in dependence upon that divine power, not human persuasion. The effectiveness of witness depends not on eloquence but on the Spirit's conviction. The gospel proclaimed with faith and humility carries supernatural authority because it is the message of the living God.

Practical Ways to Imitate Jesus in Evangelism

Imitating Jesus in evangelism involves cultivating the following Christlike characteristics and practices:

1. Compassionate Concern: See others through the eyes of Christ—broken, lost, and precious. Let compassion motivate every conversation.

2. Scriptural Foundation: Base every message on the Word of God, not human philosophy. Let "It is written" define your evangelism.

3. Personal Connection: Engage individuals personally, addressing their unique struggles and questions. Listen before speaking.

4. Bold Clarity: Speak the truth without compromise, even when it challenges popular opinion.

5. Prayerful Dependence: Begin, sustain, and conclude every effort in prayer, trusting God to work through His Word.

6. Kingdom Focus: Emphasize repentance, faith, and obedience to God's will, not emotional experience or worldly benefits.

7. Enduring Patience: Expect rejection and persevere in love, reflecting the long-suffering heart of Christ.

The Ultimate Aim: Reflecting Christ to the World

Evangelism that imitates Jesus glorifies God because it reflects His nature. The goal is not to impress with intellect or emotion but to reveal Christ through both message and manner. Paul wrote, "Be imitators of me, just as I also am of Christ" (1 Corinthians 11:1). The faithful evangelist mirrors the compassion, courage, and truthfulness of the Savior, becoming a living testimony of the gospel's power.

When believers imitate Jesus in evangelism, they become the hands, voice, and heart of God reaching into the world. Their message carries both authority and tenderness, their lives illustrate the grace they proclaim, and their faithfulness fulfills the mission entrusted by their Lord. To evangelize like Jesus is to embody His truth, extend His mercy, and invite the world to behold His glory.

APOLOGETICS 10 Imitate the Apostle Paul When Evangelizing

The Apostle Paul stands as one of the greatest examples of a faithful evangelist in all of Christian history. His life, ministry, and writings reveal an unshakable devotion to Jehovah and an unwavering commitment to the gospel of Jesus Christ. Paul's example provides a masterclass in how to proclaim the truth of salvation effectively, courageously, and compassionately. To imitate Paul when evangelizing is to follow his Christ-centered mindset, his disciplined method, and his sacrificial lifestyle—all of which were patterned after the Lord Himself. As Paul wrote, "Be imitators of me, just as I also am of Christ" (1 Corinthians 11:1).

Paul's evangelism was marked by clarity of message, boldness of spirit, and endurance under hardship. He was not driven by ambition, popularity, or comfort but by the glory of God and the salvation of souls. His zeal was balanced by humility, his knowledge by love, and his courage by dependence upon the power of the Holy Spirit. To imitate Paul, the Christian must understand not only what he said but how and why he said it.

Paul's Conviction in the Gospel

At the heart of Paul's evangelism was his absolute conviction that the gospel is the power of God unto salvation. He declared with confidence, "I am not ashamed of the gospel, for it is the power of God for salvation to everyone who believes" (Romans 1:16). Paul understood that the message of Christ crucified and risen was not one among many religious options—it was the only truth capable of reconciling man to God.

His confidence rested not in human persuasion but in divine authority. The gospel he preached was revealed "not according to man," but through Jesus Christ (Galatians 1:11–12). This conviction freed him from fear and compromise. Whether speaking before kings or prisoners, Jews or Gentiles, Paul knew that the same gospel held the same saving power for all.

To imitate Paul in evangelism is to hold the same unyielding faith in the sufficiency and supremacy of the gospel. Modern believers must reject the temptation to rely on entertainment, emotionalism, or worldly methods. The gospel itself—pure, simple, and powerful—remains the instrument by which God changes hearts.

Paul's Humility and Dependence on God

Though Paul possessed unmatched theological insight and intellectual brilliance, he approached ministry with humility. He confessed to the Corinthians, "I was with you in weakness and in fear and in much trembling" (1 Corinthians 2:3). His reliance was not on eloquence or human wisdom but on the Spirit's power, "so that your faith would not rest on the wisdom of men, but on the power of God" (1 Corinthians 2:5).

Paul's humility flowed from his awareness of grace. Once a persecutor of the church, he never forgot what he had been saved from. He wrote, "I am the least of the apostles, and not fit to be called an apostle, because I persecuted the church of God. But by the grace of God I am what I am" (1 Corinthians 15:9–10). This humility made his evangelism authentic. He did not preach as one above others but as a redeemed sinner proclaiming the same mercy he had received.

Imitating Paul means rejecting pride and embracing dependence upon God. The true evangelist recognizes that success does not come from cleverness or charisma but from the Spirit's work through the Word. The believer's role is to plant and water faithfully, trusting Jehovah to give the growth (1 Corinthians 3:6–7).

Paul's Courage and Boldness

Paul's evangelism was fearless because it was grounded in eternal truth. He faced persecution, imprisonment, stoning, and ridicule, yet his commitment never wavered. In Philippians 1:20, he expressed his unwavering goal "that Christ will even now, as always, be exalted in my body, whether by life or by death." His courage came not from self-confidence but from faith in God's sovereignty.

Paul's boldness was inseparable from his love for souls. He endured suffering because he valued eternal salvation more than temporal safety. In Acts 20:24, he declared, "I do not consider my life of any account as dear to myself, so that I may finish my course and the ministry which I received from the Lord Jesus, to testify solemnly of the gospel of the grace of God."

To imitate Paul is to evangelize with similar courage. In a culture hostile to truth, believers must be willing to suffer for the gospel without compromise. Boldness, however, must always be guided by wisdom and gentleness. Paul spoke truth firmly, but never arrogantly. His goal was not to conquer opponents but to win them to Christ.

Paul's Adaptability Without Compromise

Paul's evangelistic effectiveness was enhanced by his adaptability. He understood that different audiences required different approaches, though the message never changed. He wrote, "To the Jews I became as a Jew, so that I might win Jews; to those who are without law, as without law... I have become all things to all men, so that I may by all means save some" (1 Corinthians 9:20–22).

This flexibility was not compromise but strategy. Paul respected cultural differences while remaining anchored in truth. In synagogues, he reasoned from the Scriptures, proving that Jesus was the promised Messiah (Acts 17:2–3). Among Gentiles, he began with creation, explaining the nature of the true God (Acts 17:22–31). His adaptability showed both intellectual sensitivity and spiritual discernment.

Modern evangelists must follow this example. To imitate Paul means to know the audience, understand their worldview, and build bridges of understanding without diluting the message. The gospel must be communicated in language the listener can grasp, yet without concession to error. Like Paul, the faithful witness must meet people where they are in order to lead them where they need to be—in Christ.

Paul's Emphasis on Scripture and Reason

Paul's evangelism was always grounded in Scripture. He did not rely on philosophical speculation but on divine revelation. When addressing Jews, he "reasoned with them from the Scriptures, explaining and giving evidence that the Christ had to suffer and rise again from the dead" (Acts 17:2–3). For Paul, the Scriptures were not optional aids but the very foundation of truth.

At the same time, Paul used reason effectively. His arguments were logical, coherent, and persuasive, demonstrating that faith in Christ was both reasonable and true. In Acts 17:17, he reasoned daily in the marketplace, engaging thinkers and skeptics alike. His example teaches that reason, when submitted to revelation, is a powerful tool for evangelism.

Imitating Paul means mastering both the content and communication of the gospel. The believer must know Scripture thoroughly, think clearly, and speak persuasively. The power of truth is magnified when it is presented with clarity and conviction.

Paul's Compassionate Heart

Beneath Paul's boldness was a deeply compassionate heart. His evangelism was not driven by argument but by love. He wrote to the Thessalonians, "Having so fond an affection for you, we were pleased to impart to you not only the gospel of God but also our own lives, because you had become very dear to us" (1 Thessalonians 2:8).

Paul's compassion reflected the heart of Christ. He wept for those who rejected the gospel, saying, "I have great sorrow and unceasing grief in my heart" for his unbelieving kinsmen (Romans 9:2–3). His concern was not abstract—it was personal and profound. He longed for people to experience the same mercy that had transformed his own life.

To imitate Paul in evangelism is to love people sincerely. The apologist who argues without compassion misrepresents the gospel. Truth must be spoken in love, for love is the soil in which truth takes root. Paul's tears for the lost teach that evangelism must flow from both conviction and compassion.

Paul's Perseverance in Suffering

No evangelist suffered more for the gospel than Paul. He endured beatings, imprisonments, shipwrecks, hunger, and rejection (2 Corinthians 11:23–27). Yet through all these trials, his faith remained steadfast. He saw suffering not as failure but as participation in the mission of Christ. "For momentary, light affliction is producing for us an eternal weight of glory far beyond all comparison" (2 Corinthians 4:17).

Paul's perseverance stemmed from his eternal perspective. He knew that the reward of faithfulness far outweighed the cost. His endurance inspired others to courage, and his letters continue to strengthen believers today.

Imitating Paul means embracing hardship as part of gospel ministry. The faithful evangelist does not retreat in adversity but presses forward, knowing that Jehovah uses suffering to purify motives and magnify His grace. Perseverance authenticates faith and gives credibility to the message.

Paul's Prayerful Spirit

Paul's ministry was saturated with prayer. He prayed for open doors for the gospel (Colossians 4:3), for boldness to speak as he should (Ephesians 6:19), and for the spiritual growth of those he had led to Christ (Philippians 1:3–6). Prayer was both preparation and power for his evangelism.

He understood that conversion is a divine work. Thus, he prayed for hearts to be opened by God, as in Lydia's case, whose heart the Lord opened "to respond to the things spoken by Paul" (Acts 16:14). His prayerful dependence demonstrated his confidence that only God can bring spiritual life.

To imitate Paul is to make prayer the lifeblood of evangelism. Every conversation, sermon, or outreach effort must begin and end in prayer. Without prayer, evangelism becomes an exercise in self-reliance rather than divine partnership.

Paul's Focus on Discipleship

Paul viewed evangelism not as an isolated act but as the beginning of lifelong discipleship. He labored to establish believers in the truth and strengthen the churches he planted. His goal was not merely to make converts but to produce mature followers of Christ who could teach others (2 Timothy 2:2).

He invested personally in those he led to faith, mentoring men like Timothy and Titus to carry the work forward. This emphasis on discipleship ensured the ongoing growth and stability of the church.

Imitating Paul means committing not only to proclaim the gospel but to nurture those who respond. True evangelism continues beyond conversion, guiding new believers into obedience, fellowship, and maturity.

Paul's Focus on God's Glory

Above all, Paul's evangelism was God-centered. His driving passion was that Christ would be glorified through the salvation of souls. "For from Him and through Him and to Him are all things. To Him be the glory forever. Amen" (Romans 11:36). He did not seek personal recognition or comfort; his joy was found in seeing others reconciled to God.

His ministry motto can be summarized in Philippians 1:21: "For to me, to live is Christ and to die is gain." Every action, every sermon, every hardship flowed from this singular devotion. To imitate Paul is to make the glory of God the goal of evangelism—to preach Christ, not self, and to exalt Jehovah's name above all.

Paul's Persuasive Method and Convictional Language

Another powerful aspect of Paul's evangelistic example is his use of **persuasive, convictional language**. His ministry was not mechanical or detached—it was driven by deep personal assurance. He often used expressions such as "I am convinced," "I know," and "I am persuaded," which reveal not only intellectual certainty but heartfelt conviction born of personal experience with the risen Christ. In Romans 8:38–39, he wrote, "For I am convinced that neither death, nor life, nor angels, nor rulers, nor things present, nor things to come... will be able to separate us from the love of God, which is in Christ Jesus our Lord." This confidence infused his preaching with authority and authenticity.

Paul also made frequent use of the verb *peithō* (to persuade, to convince), demonstrating that persuasion was central to his evangelistic approach. Acts 18:4 records that he "was reasoning in the synagogue every Sabbath and trying to persuade (*peithō*) Jews and Greeks." Similarly, in Acts 28:23, he "was explaining to them by solemnly testifying about the kingdom of God and trying to persuade (*peithō*) them concerning Jesus from both the Law of Moses and the Prophets." His preaching was not passive; it actively sought to convince the mind, convict the conscience, and move the will.

This Greek term *peithō* carries a range of meaning including "to convince by argument, to win confidence, or to gain assent." Paul employed it with both intellectual rigor and spiritual sincerity. His goal was not manipulation but transformation. He reasoned logically, appealed to Scripture, and called for response, trusting the Holy Spirit to seal conviction in the listener's heart.

To imitate Paul in this regard, believers must speak with the same assurance of faith and the same desire to persuade others of truth. The apologist and evangelist should communicate with both clarity and passion, expressing personal conviction rooted in divine revelation. When the messenger himself is persuaded of the truth he proclaims, his words carry persuasive power. Like Paul, the Christian must combine knowledge with assurance, logic with love, and truth with urgency.

Paul's persuasion was not merely intellectual—it was relational and spiritual. He understood that genuine persuasion requires empathy and credibility. He persuaded not as a philosopher detached from his audience but as a servant pleading for reconciliation with God. As he wrote, "Therefore, we are ambassadors for Christ, as though God were making an appeal through us; we beg you on behalf of Christ, be reconciled to God" (2 Corinthians 5:20). This divine appeal through human persuasion remains the model for all who would imitate Paul's heart and method in evangelism.

Conclusion: Following Paul as He Followed Christ

Imitating Paul when evangelizing means imitating his faith, humility, courage, compassion, and endurance—all of which reflected his imitation of Christ. Paul's life demonstrates that effective evangelism is not a matter of method but of character. It flows from a heart transformed by grace and consumed by the desire to glorify God.

The believer who follows Paul's example will proclaim the gospel boldly, love people sincerely, and trust God completely. Like Paul, he will be able to say at the end of his life, "I have fought the good fight, I have finished the course, I have kept the faith" (2 Timothy 4:7). The legacy of Paul's evangelism continues through every Christian who faithfully carries the same message—the gospel of the grace of God—to a world still in need of redemption.

Glossary of Terms

Absolute Truth – The belief that truth is objective, universal, and grounded in the nature of God, not subject to human opinion or cultural perspective.

Ad Hominem – A logical fallacy in which an argument attacks the person making a claim rather than addressing the claim itself.

Ambassador for Christ – A title for believers representing Christ to the world through proclamation, conduct, and defense of the gospel (2 Corinthians 5:20).

Apologia (Greek) – Meaning "defense" or "reasoned statement," the biblical term that forms the basis for *apologetics* (1 Peter 3:15).

Apologetics – The reasoned defense and confirmation of the Christian faith, demonstrating its truth, rationality, and coherence with reality.

Apostasy – The act of abandoning or rejecting the faith once professed; often associated with false teaching and moral compromise.

Atheism – The worldview that denies the existence of God; refuted in the book as irrational and self-defeating since it cannot justify truth, morality, or reason.

Authority of Scripture – The teaching that the Bible is the ultimate and final standard for truth, doctrine, and moral conduct.

Biblical Apologetics (Presuppositional) – A branch of apologetics that begins with the authority of Scripture, showing that all reasoning presupposes God's revelation.

Christocentric – Having Christ as the center and focus of faith, theology, and evangelism.

Classical Apologetics – A two-step apologetic approach that first demonstrates the existence of God through reason and evidence, then confirms Christianity as true through historical and biblical proof.

Common Grace – God's benevolence shown to all humanity through creation and conscience, even apart from saving faith.

Conversion – The turning of a person from sin to faith in Christ, resulting in regeneration and reconciliation with God.

Cultural Discernment – The ability to recognize and evaluate cultural ideas and practices according to biblical truth.

Deism – The belief in a distant Creator who does not intervene in human affairs; rejected as inconsistent with biblical revelation.

Discipleship – The process of spiritual growth and obedience to Christ following conversion; the ultimate goal of evangelism.

Empirical Evidence – Observable and verifiable data used in evidential apologetics to demonstrate the reliability of Scripture and the historical truth of Christ's resurrection.

Epistemology – The study of knowledge and belief; Christian epistemology asserts that true knowledge begins with "the fear of Jehovah" (Proverbs 1:7).

Eschatology – The study of end times, including Christ's return and the final judgment; the book affirms premillennial eschatology.

Evidential Apologetics – An approach that uses historical and empirical evidence (such as fulfilled prophecy, miracles, and the resurrection) to confirm the truth of Christianity.

Evangelism – The proclamation of the gospel message of salvation through Jesus Christ, calling people to repentance and faith.

Faith – Rational trust in God and His Word, grounded in evidence and revelation rather than blind belief.

Fallacy – A flaw in reasoning that weakens an argument; apologists are warned to avoid these in defending the faith.

General Revelation – God's self-disclosure through nature, conscience, and history, making His existence evident to all people (Romans 1:20).

Gentleness and Respect – The biblical manner required of all apologists (1 Peter 3:15); truth must be spoken in love.

Gospel – The good news of salvation through the life, death, and resurrection of Jesus Christ.

Grace – God's unmerited favor given to humanity for salvation and sanctification.

Heretic / Heresy – A person or teaching that contradicts essential biblical truths; apologetics guards the church against heresy.

Historical-Grammatical Method – The proper method of interpreting Scripture by examining its original grammar, context, and authorial intent to discern literal meaning.

Holiness – Moral and spiritual purity reflecting God's character; essential to the credibility of the evangelist and apologist.

Illumination – The work of God's Spirit through Scripture that enables understanding of divine truth.

Imago Dei – Latin for "Image of God"; the biblical teaching that humanity was created to reflect God's nature and moral capacity (Genesis 1:26–27).

Inerrancy – The doctrine that Scripture is without error in all that it affirms in its original manuscripts.

Jehovah – The personal covenant name of God used throughout the book to reflect His self-revelation as the one true God.

Justification – The divine act of declaring a sinner righteous through faith in Christ alone.

Logic – The study of correct reasoning; used in apologetics to demonstrate the coherence of the Christian worldview.

Lordship of Christ – The recognition that Jesus Christ is sovereign over all areas of life, including thought, morality, and truth.

Miracle – A supernatural act of God that confirms divine truth and validates the message or messenger (e.g., Jesus' resurrection).

Monotheism – The belief in one true God; foundational to Christian theism.

Natural Revelation – Another term for general revelation—God's witness through the created order.

Objective Morality – The belief that moral truths are absolute and grounded in God's nature, not human preference.

Orthodox Christianity – The body of essential Christian doctrine consistent with the teachings of Scripture and the apostles.

Pauline Persuasion – The method of persuasion used by the Apostle Paul, combining logical reasoning (*peithō*) with spiritual conviction and compassion.

Peithō (Greek) – The verb meaning "to persuade" or "to convince," used by Paul to describe his evangelistic reasoning.

Philosophical Apologetics – The branch of apologetics dealing with ultimate questions of existence, truth, and morality through rational argumentation.

Presuppositional Apologetics – The apologetic approach that begins with the presupposition that Scripture is the ultimate authority for truth and reason.

Prophecy – Divine revelation of future events, often cited in apologetics as evidence for the Bible's inspiration and the Messiahship of Jesus.

Rational Faith – Belief that harmonizes with evidence, reason, and Scripture.

Reconciliation – The restoration of fellowship between God and man through the atoning work of Christ.

Redemption – The act of being delivered from sin's penalty and power through Christ's sacrifice.

Regeneration – The new birth wrought by God, producing spiritual life in those who believe in Christ.

Relativism – The belief that truth and morality are subjective and culturally defined; refuted throughout the book as logically self-defeating.

Repentance – A turning from sin to God in genuine sorrow and obedience.

Revelation (Divine) – God's act of making Himself known through creation (general revelation) and Scripture (special revelation).

Sanctification – The process by which believers are made holy and conformed to the image of Christ.

Scripture Sufficiency – The teaching that the Bible contains all truth necessary for salvation, faith, and obedience.

Sin – Rebellion against God and violation of His moral law; the universal human problem requiring redemption.

Soteriology – The doctrine of salvation, encompassing justification, regeneration, and sanctification.

Special Revelation – God's specific self-disclosure through His Word and through Jesus Christ.

Theism – The belief in a personal, infinite, and moral Creator who is active in His creation; contrasted with atheism, deism, and pantheism.

Trinity – The biblical doctrine that the one God eternally exists in three distinct persons: Father, Son, and Holy Spirit.

Truth – That which corresponds to reality and is consistent with God's character and revelation.

Witness – The act of testifying to the truth of Christ through word and deed.

Worldview – The comprehensive framework of beliefs through which one interprets reality; the

Christian worldview alone is consistent, moral, and true.

Worship – Reverent devotion and obedience to God in all areas of life; evangelism and apologetics are forms of worship when done for His glory.

Bibliography

Andrews, E. D. (2012). *DIFFICULTIES IN THE BIBLE UPDATED: Updated and Expanded.* Cambridge, OH: Christian Publishing House.

Andrews, E. D. (2016). *INTERPRETING THE BIBLE: Introduction to Biblical Hermeneutics.* Cambridge, OH: Christian Publishing House.

Andrews, E. D. (2016). *THE COMPLETE GUIDE to BIBLE TRANSLATION: Bible Translation Choices and Translation Principles [Second Edition] .* Cambridge: Christian Publishing House.

Andrews, E. D. (2016). *THE EVANGELISM HANDBOOK: How All Christians Can Effectively Share God's Word in Their Community, [SECOND EDITION].* Cambridge, OH: Christian Publishing House.

Andrews, E. D. (2016). *YOUR GUIDE FOR DEFENDING THE BIBLE: Self-Education of the Bible Made Easy.* Cambridge, OH: Christian Publishing House.

Andrews, E. D. (2017). *CONVERSATIONAL EVANGELISM: Defending the Faith,*

Reasoning from the Scriptures, Explaining and Proving, Instructing in Sound Doctrine, and Overturning False Reasoning [Second Edition]. Cambridge, OH: Christian Publishing House.

Andrews, E. D. (2017). *IS THE BIBLE REALLY THE WORD OF GOD?: Is Christianity the One True Faith?* Cambridge, Ohio: Christian Publishing House.

Andrews, E. D. (2017). *IS THE QURAN THE WORD OF GOD?: Is Islam the One True Faith.* Cambridge, OH: Christian Publishing House.

Andrews, E. D. (2018). *REASONING FROM THE SCRIPTURES: Sharing CHRIST as You Help Others to Learn about the Mighty works of God.* Cambridge, Ohio: Christian Publishing House.

Andrews, E. D. (2018). *REASONING WITH THE WORLD'S VARIOUS RELIGIONS: Examining and Evangelizing Other Faiths.* Cambridge, OH: Christian Publishing House.

Andrews, E. D. (2018). *The CHURCH CURE: Overcoming Church Problems.* Cambridge, OH: Christian Publishing House.

Andrews, E. D. (2019). *MIRACLES: What Does the Bible Really Teach?* Cambridge, OH: Christian Publishing House.

Andrews, E. D. (2022). *THE QUEST FOR THE HISTORICAL JESUS: Are Doubts About Jesus Justified?* Cambridge, OH: Christian Publishing House.

Andrews, E. D. (2023). *BIBLICAL EXEGESIS: Biblical Criticism on Trial.* Cambridge, OH: Christian Publishing House.

Andrews, E. D. (2023). *CHRISTIAN APOLOGETICS: Answering the Tough Questions: Evidence and Reason in Defense of the Faith.* Cambridge, Ohio: Christian Publishing House.

Andrews, E. D. (2023). *HOW WE GOT THE BIBLE.* Cambridge, OH: Christian Publishing House.

Andrews, E. D. (2023). *ISLAM & THE QURAN: Examining the Quran & Islamic Teachings.* Cambridge, OH: Christian Publishing House.

Andrews, E. D. (2023). *ISLAMIC ESCHATOLOGY: Awaiting Al-Mahdi—The Twelfth Imam and the Future of Islam.* Cambridge, OH: Christian Publishing House.

Andrews, E. D. (2023). *THE BIBLE ON TRIAL: Examining the Evidence for Being Inspired, Inerrant, Authentic, and True.* Cambridge, Ohio: Christian Publishing House.

Andrews, E. D. (2023). *UNSHAKABLE BELIEFS: Strategies for Strengthening and Defending Your Faith.* Cambridge, OH: Christian Publishing House.

Andrews, E. D. (2024). *BATTLE PLANS: A Game Plan for Answering Objections to the Christian Faith.* Cambridge, OH: Christian Publishing House.

Andrews, E. D. (2024). *CREATION AND COSMOS: A Journey Through Creation, Science, and the Origins of Life.* Cambridge, OH: Christian Publishing House.

Andrews, E. D. (2024). *FAITH UNDER FIRE: Refuting the Top 30 Arguments Atheists Make Against Christianity.* Cambridge, OH: Christian Publishing House.

Andrews, E. D. (2024). *REASON MEETS FAITH: Addressing and Refuting Atheism's Challenges to Christianity.* Cambridge, OH: Christian Publishing House.

Andrews, E. D. (2024). *THE ENCYCLOPEDIA OF CHRISTIAN APOLOGETICS: The Resource for Pastors, Teachers, and Believers.* Cambridge: Christan Publishing House.

Andrews, E. D. (2024). *THE HISTORICAL ADAM & EVE: Reconciling Faith and Fact in Genesis.* Cambridge, OH: Christian Publishing House.

Andrews, E. D. (2024). *THE HISTORICAL JESUS: The Death, Burial, and Resurrection of Jesus Christ.* Cambridge, OH: Christian Publishing House.

Andrews, E. D. (2025). *ATHEISM: What Will You Say to an Atheist.* Cambridge, OH: Christian Publising House.

Andrews, E. D. (2025). *BIBLE DIFFICULTIES: How to Approach Difficulties In the Bible.* Cambridge, OH: Christian Publishing House.

Andrews, E. D. (2025). *BIBLICAL WORDS AND THEIR MEANING: An Introduction to Lexical Semantics.* Cambridge, OH: Christian Publishing House.

Andrews, E. D. (2025). *CAN WE TRUST THE BIBLE?* Cambridge, OH: Christian Publishing House.

Andrews, E. D. (2025). *DISCOVERING GENESIS ANSWERS: Exploring the Historical and Cultural Contexts of Genesis, One Insight at a Time (Answers from Genesis).* Cambridge, OH: Christian Publishing House.

Andrews, E. D. (2025). *DISCOVERING GENESIS ANSWERS: Tackling Tough Questions in Genesis: One Solution at a Time (Answers from Genesis).* Cambridge, OH: Christian Publishing House.

Andrews, E. D. (2025). *DISCOVERING GENESIS ANSWERS: Unveiling the Truths of Creation, One Answer at a Time (Answers from Genesis).* Cambridge, OH: Chritian Publishing House.

Andrews, E. D. (2025). *ISLAMIC IDEOLOGICAL JIHAD: Islamic-Funded, Islamic-Indoctrinated, Western Youth.* Cambridge, OH: Christian Publishing House.

Andrews, E. D. (2025). *LINGUISTICS AND THE BIBLICAL TEXT: Unlocking Scripture Through the Science of Language.* Cambridge, OH: Christian Publishing House.

Andrews, E. D. (2025). *OVERCOMING BIBLE DIFFICULTIES: Answers to the So-Called*

Errors and Contradictions [Second Edition]. Cambridge: Christian Publishing House.

Andrews, E. D. (2025). *PROVING GOD'S EXISTENCE.* Cambridge, OH: Christian Publishing House.

Andrews, E. D. (2025). *THE FACES OF ISLAM: Faith or Facade: Decoding Islam's Strategies.* Cambridge, OH: Christian Publishing House.

Andrews, E. D. (2025). *UNDERSTANDING BIBLICAL WORDS: A Guide to Sound Interpretation.* Cambridge, OH: Christian Publishing House.

Andrews, E. D. (2025). *WONDERFULLY MADE: Wonderful Are God's Works.* Cambridge, OH: Christian Publishing House.